Land Rover Discovery

Land Rover

Discovery

1989 – 1998

James Taylor

MOTOR RACING PUBLICATIONS LTD
Unit 6, The Pilton Estate, 46 Pitlake, Croydon CR0 3RY, England

First published 1999

British Library Cataloguing in Publication Data

Taylor, James, 1950-
    Land Rover Discovery : 1989-1998
    1. Rover automobile – History 2. Rover automobile – Design and construction
        3. Rover automobile – Handling characteristics 4. Rover automobile – Purchasing
    I. Title
    629.2'222

ISBN 1899870 40 7

Typesetting and origination by Jack Andrews Design, Croydon, Surrey

Printed in Great Britain by The Amadeus Press Ltd, Huddersfield, West Yorkshire

Contents

Introduction and acknowledgements

I missed the launch of the Discovery in 1989, but thanks to Land Rover Ltd I was able to catch up on their new product very soon afterwards at an off-road driving day held at Eastnor Castle. Since then, I have been lucky enough to attend both the launch of the second-generation vehicle in 1994 and that of the New Discovery in 1998, as well as to borrow a selection of examples of the marque for extended assessment.

All these experiences have convinced me that the Discovery is not only an excellent everyday car, but also a first-rate off-road performer in the very best Land Rover tradition. Its appeal extends to suburban housewives and four-wheel drive enthusiasts alike because it is such a versatile and capable vehicle. The sophistication of the latest models makes the earliest examples seem positively crude by comparison, but that does not make them any less practical.

I have been writing about the Discovery ever since it was announced, most notably in *Land Rover Owner* magazine, for which much of the research behind this book was originally done. Some parts of Chapters 10 and 11 first appeared in my earlier MRP book, *Land Rover Discovery – The Enthusiast's Companion*, but of course the whole text has been thoroughly revised and updated. The Discovery is sold in 125 countries worldwide, and it has not always been possible to keep pace with every special edition and variant which has been introduced in all of those markets. However, I have provided details in the text whenever they have been available to me.

Over the years, I have also been able to interview many of the people involved with the design, manufacture and marketing of the Discovery. All of them have made their own enthusiastic contributions to the story which is told in this new book, and I hope the finished product does not distort the truth which they tried to explain to me. In particular, I must single out Tim Ackerley (marketing), Paul Adkin (diesel engines), John Bilton (product planning), Mike Donovan (Jay project leader), David Evans (styling), Colin Green (brand manager) and Bill Morris (Engineering Director). My sincere thanks also go to all those enthusiasts and owners who have helped out along the way.

James Taylor

The cover illustrations are reproduced by kind permission of *Land Rover World* and *Off Road & 4 Wheel Drive* magazines.

Historical note

Land Rover was originally a trademark of the Rover Company, an independent car manufacturer based after 1945 at Solihull, in Warwickshire. In 1966, the Rover Company joined the Leyland Motors combine, which already owned Standard-Triumph and was itself an established truck and bus manufacturer.

In 1968, the British Government fostered a merger between Leyland and British Motor Holdings, itself only recently formed from the amalgamation of BMC (Austin, Morris, MG, Riley and Wolseley) with Jaguar (which also owned Daimler and Guy). The result was the British Leyland Motor Corporation, most commonly known by its short name of British Leyland or BL. At this point, Land Rover became one of the many BL marques. BL moved into Government ownership in 1975.

Three years later, in 1978, Land Rover became a separate company for the first time when Land Rover Ltd was established as an operating division of British Leyland. During 1982, BL was renamed the Austin Rover Group, and from 1986 it was re-organized as the Rover Group. In 1988, the Rover Group was sold to British Aerospace, which sold it on again to BMW in 1994. Land Rover is now one of four marques within the Rover Group (the other three being Rover, Mini and MG), which is in turn part of the BMW Group.

CHAPTER 1

GENESIS

The origins of the Discovery

The Land Rover Discovery was introduced in 1989 after being designed and developed in a time short enough to break industry records. It was an immediate and massive success, receiving critical acclaim from expert journalists and 4x4 enthusiasts worldwide and claiming for Land Rover the lion's share of a market in which the company had not even been represented before.

This success was absolutely critical to the survival of Land Rover, which had been sinking fast during the early 1980s after a period of complacency in the 1970s. The profits generated by the Discovery were ploughed back into improved products and helped to fund the design and development of the Freelander, introduced as a fourth model-range in 1997. It was anticipated that during 1998 Land Rover would build close on 200,000 vehicles whereas 10 years earlier it had managed fewer than 46,000.

The origins of a problem

To understand this success story properly, it is necessary to go back more than a decade before the Discovery was announced, to the dark days of the 1970s when Land Rover's owners, British Leyland, were the butt of every British comedian's jokes. British Leyland had been established in 1968, when the Government had persuaded the two big groupings of British motor manufacturers to amalgamate in order to stave off foreign competition. Its problem was that as a company it was too large and unwieldy, and it embraced too many formerly rival marques. While its management struggled to sort out the internal conflicts which arose as a result, the Land Rover marque was left well alone because it competed with nothing else and was selling strongly.

Unfortunately, all the profits which accrued from the strong sales of Land Rover utilities and Range Rovers were diverted to shore up the loss-making Austin-Morris volume cars division. As a result, Land Rover production was not stepped up to meet the huge demand – mainly from overseas, where 75 per cent of its vehicles were sold – and other manufacturers saw their opportunity to sell rival products. Nor was any significant amount of money pumped into new model development, with the result that new vehicles from other manufacturers began to make the Land Rover products look outdated.

Solution and setback

After British Leyland's financial collapse in late 1974 and its subsequent rescue by the British Government, a report on the company's future was commissioned from industrial adviser Lord Ryder. Among the Ryder recommendations was that a major investment should be made in the Land Rover marque, and that this should be operated as a separate business unit. So in 1978, Land Rover Ltd was established with a budget of £280 million to be spent on securing its future.

The first fruits of the new budget were seen in 1979, when the long-wheelbase Land Rover gained a V8 engine option and some important upgrades were made to the Range Rover. The next step was to move Rover car manufacture out of the Solihull site and turn the whole area over to 4x4 manufacture from early 1982. At the same time, new plant was built to manufacture larger numbers of Land Rovers and Range Rovers. Money went into new products, too: from 1981, a four-door Range Rover joined the existing two-door model; from 1983, the new coil-sprung Land Rover One Ten replaced the old leaf-sprung long-wheelbase model; and from 1984 the new Ninety replaced

Before the Discovery the Land Rover name was associated with rugged utilities like this Series III 88-inch soft-top, built in the mid-1970s.

the short-wheelbase version.

Yet just as Land Rover was gearing up to produce more and better vehicles to meet demand its major markets started to collapse. The Australian market had already been lost to

African market lost to cheaper Japanese 4x4s

the Toyota Land Cruiser during the 1970s, when Land Rover had been unable to provide a properly competitive product. Now, as the 1980s opened, the traditional Land Rover stronghold

of Africa also went to the Japanese. One reason was that the British Government changed the overseas aid arrangements which had previously encouraged African governments to buy British. Another was that the Japanese manufacturers, expanding their exports rapidly during the 1970s, had quickly spotted that Land Rover was unable to meet demand from Africa and had developed cheaper 4x4 vehicles for that market. Things went from bad to worse, and 1983 and 1984 were the company's worst-ever trading years, with a combined loss of around £40 million.

A new market
The Japanese manufacturers had also begun to exploit the potential of a new market, again at Land Rover's expense. The Range Rover had been a huge hit during the 1970s, and yet its running costs and purchase price had put it out of reach of many potential buyers. Identifying a large proportion of these buyers as family men

and women in the developed countries who saw in Land Rover's flagship an alternative to a conventional estate car, the Japanese manufacturers designed cheaper 4x4 estate models to suit them.

During 1981, Isuzu introduced the Trooper and Mitsubishi the Pajero (called the Shogun in Britain), and these models found a ready market. Backed up by short-wheelbase models aimed at those with an outdoor lifestyle, they really started the four-wheel-drive boom in the developed countries, selling to a market where Land Rover was simply unable to compete. It was neither the traditional 4x4 utility market nor the expensive luxury 4x4 market, but somewhere in between. In later years, it would be categorized by marketing specialists as the Personal Transport Sector of the 4x4 market.

A new strategy

By the end of 1982, Land Rover was in trouble. Sales had collapsed in its largest overseas markets, and there was no doubt that it would take several millions of pounds and a good number of years even to regain its competitive edge against the latest Japanese 4x4 utilities. Equally, its credibility as a major player in the four-wheel-drive market was being threatened by the fact that it was not competing in the new family 4x4 sector opened up by the Trooper and Pajero. This was crisis time, and when new Managing Director Tony Gilroy arrived from British Leyland's Freight Rover van division in January 1983, it was clear what his priority must be.

Gilroy initiated a ground-up review of Land Rover's products and markets. His predecessor as Managing Director, Mike Hodgkinson, had already sketched out plans for streamlining the manufacturing operation by closing satellite factories and centralizing production at Solihull, and Gilroy accelerated this process. Even before the report on the major review had been completed, however, certain things had become clear. It would be far too costly and risky to try to regain Land Rover's lost markets for utility vehicles in the developing countries. Instead, the company should focus on selling vehicles in the developed countries, and should do so by improving its Range Rover luxury

From 1979 new investment allowed Land Rover to replace the ageing six-cylinder engine which was optional in the long (109-inch) wheelbase models with the ex-Buick V8. This is a 1981-model Stage 1 V8 with the popular Station Wagon body.

Land Rover's flagship after 1970 was the Range Rover – though relatively few people realized it was built by the same company that built the utility models! This is a 1986-model four-door Vogue, then top of the range. The Range Rover set standards for others to emulate, but it was expensive.

Range Rover technology – coil springs and permanent four-wheel drive – reached the utility models in 1983 when the Land Rover One Ten replaced the Series III long-wheelbase and Stage 1 V8 models.

product. The major targets would be Europe and the USA.

By the time the report was completed early in 1986, one other recommendation was quite clear. This was that Land Rover should develop a third product line to compete with the Japanese family 4x4s, to sell in volumes larger than either the Land Rover utilities or the Range Rover, and to generate the profits which would enable the company to develop further new products and to keep ahead of its rivals. The major demand for this new product was expected to come from Europe and the other developed countries. From this firm recommendation grew the vehicle which would be launched as the Discovery some three years later.

Budget

There was no doubt that the three-model strategy was a sound one, but its implementation would not be straightforward. Firstly, Land Rover was in no position to finance a major new project, and secondly, the company needed the new model quickly in order to ensure its very survival. So the idea was born that the third model range should be based on existing hardware in order to minimize both cost and development time.

The Land Rover chassis was clearly not suitable as a base, because the Ninety was too small and the One Ten too large for the Personal Transport market. The 100-inch wheelbase of the Range Rover chassis, however, was exactly right. Product Planner John Bilton remembers that at first there was considerable resistance to the idea of using the Range Rover chassis. Many people thought it would be too costly (but were won over when they realized that manufacturing costs would be reduced drastically through increased production volumes), while others were afraid that Range Rover sales would suffer if its chassis was used for a cheaper vehicle. This group preferred the idea of basing the new mid-range model on the chassis of the proposed Land Rover replacement, which was known as the Inca project.

Official channels

What became known as the Gilroy review was already circulating in draft form before Gilroy himself ever got to see it, and there were those at Land Rover who enthusiastically espoused the idea of a new vehicle based on the Range Rover chassis. Among them was Tim Ackerley, who was then Marketing Director. He formally put the idea of a Range Rover-based vehicle to the Product Policy Committee as early as December 6, 1985 in the guise of an Interim Model Strategy. The idea was accepted for further consideration.

However, Tony Gilroy was not a man to be rushed. In the early months of 1986 he read through the final version of the review he had commissioned and considered the options. In due course, he pronounced himself in favour of the three-model strategy and, determined to be thorough, he established a six-man team called the Swift Group to examine how Land Rover should best create a new mid-range model. At this stage, the project was given the code-name of Jay, the Range Rover-based idea becoming Jay One and the Inca-based project Jay Two.

The Swift Group started work in May 1986 and took 13 weeks to prepare its report. Meanwhile, Tim Ackerley had managed to win support for his Interim Model Strategy from key members of the Engineering, Manufacturing and Product Planning departments. Working without official sanction, these individuals had

The vehicles which established the family 4x4 market were announced in 1981 by Japanese manufacturers. This is the Mitsubishi Shogun (Pajero in most markets) in long-wheelbase guise with 2.6-litre petrol engine . . .

13

. . . and this is the strong-selling Isuzu Trooper. Both models also had short-wheelbase variants which were aimed at younger buyers with less need of their carrying capacity . . .

. . . and this is the five-door Trooper version.

developed the concept to quite an advanced stage even before the Swift Group announced that it favoured the Range Rover-derived Jay One proposal for the new vehicle. As a result, a full-size clay model of Jay came together very quickly and was ready to be presented to the Rover Group Main Board as early as September 1986! Senior managers at Land Rover were on tenterhooks for the last few months of that year, because the Jay proposal was competing for funds with a proposed new MG sports car, but the Rover Board gave its backing to Land Rover's proposal and the MG project was scrapped.

One of the key factors in securing the Rover Board's backing was that Land Rover's proposal included some innovative working methods which would ensure that the project was completed very quickly indeed by the standards of the day. The Swift Group had already demonstrated that a multi-disciplinary team approach saved time, and so Land Rover proposed to adopt a similar approach for Project Jay. Engineers, interior stylists and body and exterior stylists would all start work simultaneously and would keep one another constantly informed of progress. This Project Team method of working was quite different from the traditional motor industry style, in which one specialist group finished its work before another one started, and it dramatically shortened the vehicle's development time as well as reducing time-wasting conflicts between different design areas.

The Jay Project Team was formally established at the end of 1986 under Mike Donovan, who had also been a member of the Swift Group. In addition to designers and engineers, it contained marketing people who ran a continuous programme of further surveys over the next two and a half years to make sure that the market foreseen in 1986 did not change. Telephone interviews in the UK, Europe, Indonesia, Australia and the USA were followed by some concentrated market research in Europe and the UK and by customer clinics in those two market areas. In this way, Land Rover was as confident as it could be that it had the Jay vehicle exactly right when it was launched in the autumn of 1989.

The Ninety, smaller brother of the One Ten, replaced the 88-inch Series III types in 1984. This is a 1989-model County Station Wagon; before the Discovery, the de luxe County models were Land Rover's only response to the flood of Japanese 4x4 family estates.

CHAPTER 2

PROJECT JAY

Design, development and prototypes

The fundamental dimensions of the Jay vehicle were dictated by its Range Rover chassis, from which the self-levelling strut was deleted to help differentiate the two vehicles. The Range Rover's 3.5-litre petrol V8, five-speed manual gearbox, transfer box, axles and suspension could also be retained, but they would have to be supplemented by a modern diesel engine because buyer preference in Europe was overwhelmingly for diesels.

The obvious choice for this new engine was Gemini, the code-name for a direct-injection development of an existing diesel, on which work had already begun. The Jay Project Team scooped this up as ideal for their new vehicle, but it was at an early stage of development and there was a chance that it would not be ready in time for the Jay deadline. So contingency plans were made to use the 2.4-litre VM turbodiesel which was already earmarked for the Range Rover. In fact, it was touch and go right up to the last minute, and the Gemini engine was not finally signed off for production until the early months of 1989.

Engine development
As early as 1984, it had been clear that Land Rover would have to re-orientate itself towards the European market, and as the existing Land Rover diesel engine was an elderly design and unsuitable for high-speed car-type use, it was imperative to develop a new diesel engine.

In practice, the Product Planners working for Alan Edis at Solihull came up with three proposals. The first was that the existing four-cylinder diesel (already being enlarged to 2.5 litres) should be turbocharged to improve its road performance. This became Project Falcon. The second proposal was that the existing project – code-named Beaver – to dieselize the

Range Rover with the VM engine should go ahead as planned. These two would take care of the short-term needs. For the longer term, the existing 2.5-litre engine should be further developed by replacing its cast-iron, indirect-injection cylinder head with a new aluminium alloy direct-injection design. This would be called Project Gemini.

This powertrain strategy had been drawn up by John Bilton in Alan Edis' department. As a Product Planner, part of his job was to keep abreast of developments in motor industry technology, and he knew that Audi, Fiat and Ford were already working on small-capacity direct-injection diesels. Although much more fuel-efficient than indirect-injection systems, direct-injection types had traditionally been reserved for large slow-revving truck and bus diesels because they were very noisy – unacceptably so for the high-speed diesels needed in smaller passenger vehicles and vans. However, the news that other major manufacturers had begun to take direct injection seriously for smaller-capacity high-speed engines suggested that solutions to the existing problems might be within reach.

Both Alan Edis and Tony Gilroy were fully supportive of Bilton's suggestion to investigate direct injection, and work started on the Gemini project late in 1984. At this stage, Land Rover actually intended that it should embrace three engines – a naturally-aspirated diesel, a turbocharged version, and a petrol equivalent of the naturally-aspirated engine, using a modified version of the new direct-injection cylinder head with bowl-in-crown pistons. This commonality was expected to save on tooling costs while giving the maximum benefit to the company in terms of new engine options. As the existing 2.5-litre cylinder block would be retained, the

Early thoughts were heavily influenced by the current Japanese vehicles. The external spare wheel, split rear door and wheelarch shapes on this sketch all suggest the Isuzu Trooper. Note the smooth roof contours, again borrowed from the high-roof versions of Japanese estates. Even the side stripe suggests Japanese influence, though the '100' reflects the chosen wheelbase in inches.

Groping towards a solution: this stepped-roof style was more individual . . .

. . . although there was little doubt it had been influenced by the long-wheelbase version of the Daihatsu Fourtrak.

The first full-size clay models had the stepped-roof proposal on one side . . .

older Land Rover four-cylinder engines could also remain in production for as long as they were needed.

While Bill Morris, then Land Rover's Director of Engineering, concentrated on delivering Beaver and Falcon, a lot of the initial feasibility work on Gemini was done by John Bilton. He identified potential component suppliers and carried out preliminary negotiations with them. The Audi development work was being done in conjunction with the established specialists AVL, based at Graz, in Austria, and Land Rover

100bhp target for new turbo-diesel engine

discovered that they were working in tandem with Bosch as the component supplier. An approach to both companies secured their agreement to work with Solihull on the Gemini project, while in Britain Lucas-CAV agreed to put up a proposal to meet Land Rover's requirements. In the event, the British proposal was less promising than the joint proposal from

Germany and Austria, so Land Rover went ahead with AVL and Bosch.

Getting serious

Bill Morris now assembled his project team in the Engineering Department. Les Wilkins was recruited from Leyland Trucks, and he brought with him invaluable experience of direct-injection diesel engines. He was despatched to AVL, where he became Land Rover's link-man on the project. Back at Solihull, John Barnett and Tony Robinson made up the rest of the team, and work went ahead with all speed. Intercoolers were now accepted as a requirement to improve both fuel consumption and performance in diesel engines, so one was planned into the project. The Gemini team's initial design aims were to achieve 100bhp in the turbocharged engine (the Falcon engine would have 85bhp) with a 15 per cent improvement in fuel consumption over the indirect-injection type.

The Falcon engine was announced in October 1986, and its immediate and enthusiastic acceptance made two things clear to Land Rover. The first was that the future really did lie with diesel power if Europe was to be the target, and the second was that there would be no need for either the naturally-aspirated Gemini diesel or for the petrol version of the engine. So the plans for both engines – which had not

. . . and the sloping-roof proposal on the other, by now with Alpine lights. The style eventually chosen used elements of both proposals. This full-size clay probably dates from late 1986.

progressed beyond drawing-board and discussion – were abandoned during 1987.

Meanwhile, another important sea-change had taken place at Solihull. The Gemini engine had originally been planned as part of a cross-range engine strategy, but after Project Jay (the Discovery) was given the go-ahead in the middle of 1986, it became very closely associated with that. Land Rover now planned to launch it in Discovery first, and this put a tight deadline on the project because Discovery had to be ready for launch in mid-1989 if Land Rover was to meet its business targets. Each new setback on the project – and there were some, despite the excellent progress that was made – caused palpitations at Solihull, where a plan already existed for the VM turbodiesel to understudy Gemini. If Gemini was not ready in time, the Discovery would be launched with the VM engine, although the extra cost would have dealt a severe blow to Land Rover's hopes of pricing the Discovery competitively.

On test

All this lent an extra sense of purpose to the Gemini project. Prototypes were already achieving excellent results on emissions work and were delivering performance well in excess of expectations. After Solihull representatives drove the Ninety which AVL were using as a test-bed in Austria, all parties agreed to upgrade the design targets to reflect this exceptional progress. The maximum power requirement was raised from 100bhp to just over 111bhp, and the maximum torque from 180lb.ft to 195lb.ft. Fuel economy, already expected to be 15 per cent better than the Falcon engine's, was proving to be outstanding.

Next came a batch of 100 or so production-specification test engines. Bench-testing of up to 1,350 hours per unit had begun by the middle

Flat-out for 50,000 miles on road test

of 1987, and examples were on endurance and high-speed road-proving tests by the end of the year. Land Rover had developed a demanding road-proving test of 50,000 miles at full speed, usually run in southern Italy, and data from the Beaver and Falcon projects which had already been through this process provided valuable comparisons during the Gemini tests. By this

19

Interior styling evolved gradually, and this wallboard showed a number of proposals.

Struggling to attain a stylish and contemporary feel, the styling department came up with this among other interior proposals.

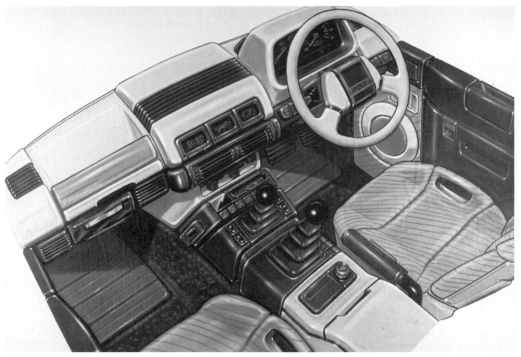

stage, Gemini engines were on test in Range Rovers as well as in Land Rovers, and examples were run in both the UK and Europe, while hot-climate testing went ahead in Arizona and cold-climate testing in Canada. Before entering production, Gemini engines had racked up 2 million road-test miles.

The real key to the success of the Gemini project was the two-stage injectors, which allowed the rate of injection to be controlled more carefully, which in turn allowed the rate of rise of combustion pressure to be managed and the characteristic diesel 'knock' to be reduced. They also had a beneficial effect on fuel

economy. The original concept of these injectors was AVL's, although the concept was slightly modified by Bosch in order to achieve consistent reliability in mass-production.

AVL was also responsible for the combustion chamber design of the new direct-injection cylinder head, and this was a further important factor in achieving excellent fuel economy and in reducing combustion noise. For its manufacture, Land Rover invested in the latest CNC (computer-controlled) machining technology – a remarkably flexible resource which could be more readily adapted to meet changes than older machine tools. Gemini proved to be Land Rover's first major use of CNC, although in fact a pilot scheme had already been running for the manufacture of some components for the V8 petrol engines.

Meanwhile, the original plan to use the block of the existing 2.5-litre diesel engine had gradually become unworkable. Minor modifications to make the engine suitable for installation in the Range Rover-based Jay vehicle turned into major ones, and in the end the block became quite different, even though it could still be machined on the same transfer lines at Solihull. According to Bill Morris, the Gemini designers got away with this – which was strictly outside the terms of the project, and therefore had no budget – by describing them internally as running modifications to the older block! The crankshaft, too, ended up being redesigned for Gemini, although to keep manufacturing costs down, the new and stronger crank was also fitted to the older 2.5-litre diesels when Gemini came on-stream.

Ready to go

By 1988, the engineering work on Gemini had progressed to the certification phase. Careful planning with Bosch had ensured consistency in the fuel injection performance, and emissions test results comfortably met the existing European standards. Although it was quite clear by this stage that Gemini had been an outstanding success as a project, the final decision that it should go into production for Discovery was not made until early in 1989 – some six or seven months before the vehicle was planned to go on sale. Pilot-production began in the spring and the engine was received with enormous enthusiasm when Discovery was announced in September. For public consumption, it was called the 200Tdi: 200

Raised-roof styling becomes Discovery feature

being the approximate maximum torque figure in lb.ft and Tdi standing for Turbocharged, Direct-injection, Intercooled.

Exterior styling

While the engineers were working on powertrain development, the stylists were busily developing the basic ideas of the full-size clay constructed in September 1986. This had already incorporated many of the distinctive features of the eventual production Discovery,

Prototypes were out on the roads during 1988 and this one went to Australia for hot-climate testing. Note the GRP 'bread van' body cladding and the GRP wheel covers designed to make it look like a Range Rover.

including the stepped roofline, large glass areas, strong bodyside styling features with an upswept D-pillar and the one-piece rear door. Further refinement of the design followed, and the basic styling was signed off in February 1987. From then on, only detail changes were made to the body.

The exterior styling, all done at Solihull, was influenced by a number of factors. Most important was the need to make the vehicle look fashionably distinctive and as different as possible from the Range Rover. A further major influence was the need to incorporate seven seats in the family-oriented models. The extra pair would have to be occasional seats in the load area at the back, but here they would be directly above the fuel tank of the Range Rover chassis, which set them unacceptably high in a standard-height body.

So to provide adequate headroom, Land Rover decided to go for a raised roof. Some Japanese 4x4 estates were already available with an optional high roof, sloping up towards the rear, and drawings were done showing a similar style on the Discovery. However, this made the vehicle look too cumbersome, and in the end the more stylish solution chosen by Daihatsu for their Fourtrak model was adopted instead. This was to use a standard-height roof at the front but to step the roofline up behind the B-pillar to give the necessary height in the rear. The Land

Rover stylists made it distinctively their own by adding to the sides of the roof the Alpine lights which had for many years been characteristic of their own utility Station Wagons.

There was also a certain amount of *trompe l'oeil* in the Jay exterior styling. Not only did it have to look different from the Range Rover, but it also had to look like the junior model. The stepped roofline actually made it a bigger vehicle, which to many eyes would have contradicted its junior status. So the rear of the body was styled to be as nearly vertical as possible, to give the impression that the Jay vehicle was shorter than the Range Rover. The trick worked well, and it would be many years before the public at large realized that the Range Rover was actually smaller than Jay – and lighter, too!

Cost-saving was also an important influence on the styling. The Japanese 4x4 estates all came in sporty short-wheelbase and family-oriented long-wheelbase forms, so Land Rover knew they had to have two models. However, they decided to put both versions on the same 100-inch wheelbase chassis to avoid the cost and complication of having two chassis. They also chose to use the same body construction as the Range Rover's, with unstressed aluminium alloy panels bolted to a steel skeleton frame. Production engineering demanded one important difference, however: the large roof

This prototype went to Canada for cold-climate testing. Note how the 'bread van' body cladding could be lifted off, and that it had cutouts for the two sunroofs underneath.

The Gemini engine was crucial to the concept of Project Jay. This cutaway example did the rounds of motor shows in 1992, and was pictured by Peter Hobson at that year's Moscow show. The turbocharger is mounted low down on the side nearer the camera.

panel would have lacked rigidity if made of alloy, so it was pressed in steel and welded to the frame.

The sporty and family-oriented body styles were previewed on opposite sides of a full-size clay model which was scooped by the motoring press during 1988 – although most commentators were confused about what it was. Most thought it was called Project J (an understandable mis-hearing of Jay), some thought it was a new Range Rover, and others believed it was some sort of mini-Range Rover. No-one of course yet knew that the two-door version would be known as a three-door and the four-door as a five-door when the vehicle was launched. These terms were chosen by the Land Rover Marketing Department and were mainly designed to help reinforce the difference between the Jay vehicle and the Range Rover, which came with either two or four doors. The public justification was that the big side-opening tailgate counted as an additional door!

The need to save costs affected areas of detail, too, so the headlamps were Freight Rover Sherpa van items, while the tail-lamps came from the Austin Maestro van. The shape of these lamps in fact brought about the distinctive chamfer on the rear of the body, between the side and rear panels. Very early production models actually carried Maestro van rear lamps, with the Austin Rover Group symbol on their lenses, but Land Rover quickly got their own version into production, with the oval Land Rover logo moulded into the plastic. Alloy wheels like those on the Range Rover would

have cost too much, so steel wheels with styled cutouts were specified for the first vehicles.

Interior design

The Swift Group had identified interior design as of major importance in attracting buyers to the new vehicle and had recommended that the Jay Team should develop complete and totally integrated interior concepts before any detail work was carried out. This was quite different from the traditional approach to interior design, in which the driver's environment is developed before the rest of the interior. In order to have the maximum number of fresh ideas to choose from, Land Rover engaged the services of two

Three teams compete to create interior design

outside design consultancies. From the automotive world they chose IAD, of Worthing, and from the world of consumer design they chose Conran Design. A third line of thinking came from their own styling studios. The brief given to all three design groups was to create a unique interior which was distinct from both traditional 4x4 and car designs, yet incorporated clear 4x4 cues and car levels of comfort.

By March 1987 the Jay Team favoured a

proposal submitted by Conran Design and a modified version of this was prepared by the Land Rover styling studio. Over the next year or so, the design was refined to suit safety, engineering, production and homologation criteria, and the Conran interior, with its distinctive Sonar Blue colour and dimpled 'golf-ball' textures, was signed off for production in the early months of 1988. However, the finished version had undoubtedly received more input from the Land Rover styling studio than was acknowledged at the Discovery's launch in 1989: the design of the inward-facing rear seats, for example, was entirely done at Solihull.

Perhaps most important was that the interior design made maximum use of the space inside the vehicle created by the raised roof. The roof above the front seats was actually slightly higher than its Range Rover equivalent, so the designers fitted map stowage pockets above the sun-visors. They added stowage nets to the slope of the stepped roof, where rear seat passengers could use them. They designed door trims with deep bins and ensured that the dashboard was

---

From design to manufacture in under 17 months

---

flat and made much better use of the space available than its Range Rover equivalent. As the two extra rear seats were to be optional, they designed deep stowage bins to fit in their place when the seats were not specified. And they enhanced the light and airy feel of the interior, which resulted from the Alpine lights, by designing not one but a pair of optional glass sunroofs.

Speed
Translating design into reality was achieved with remarkable speed thanks to the use of Computer Aided Design. Components were not tested in prototype form in the traditional way, then refined until test results were satisfactory, but instead were 'tested' by the computer before they had even been made. Adjustments were then made to the design on the basis of the computer test results, and production tooling was made as soon as the computer was happy with the design. As a result, all the Jay prototypes except the first few hand-built examples which appeared at the end of 1987

were built with production components. So successful was this procedure that only a tiny number of components had to be redesigned when prototype testing – 'validation' of the design – showed up failures.

So the first off-tools body panels were manufactured in January 1988, less than 17 months after the Jay Project had been given the go-ahead by the Rover Board. By this stage, the members of the Jay Team were already highly motivated, and were disinclined to let a strike at the Land Rover works deflect them from their aim. Mike Donovan remembers that the first off-tools bodies were actually assembled by the Jay Team itself and smuggled through the picket-lines out of the plant to be painted elsewhere!

Prototypes
In total, more than 50 prototypes would be built before the Jay vehicle was signed-off for production. The first group of prototypes was used for validation of the design, and all were hand-built by engineering fitters. The second group was distinguished by its greater number of off-tools parts and was built on the production line by assembly workers, thus validating manufacturability, processes and facilities. Both groups included petrol and turbodiesel examples, and vehicles from both groups were crash-tested at MIRA.

Some went out on the roads, wearing GRP disguise panels which gave them the appearance (from a distance, anyway) of a Range Rover van, and among these were a blue vehicle which went to Australia for hot-climate testing and a white one which went to Canada for cold-climate work. Several prototypes were registered for road use in Britain, where they received C-prefix and D-prefix number-plates dating from 1985 and 1986 to avoid attracting attention. The deception was compounded in some cases by the registration documents, which described them as Austin Maestros! Meanwhile, accessories which Land Rover Parts planned to offer for the vehicle were included in the main validation programme.

The last stage in the prototype process was the production of between 20 and 25 pilot-production vehicles in the early part of 1989. These were known as SDVs (Specially Designated Vehicles) and were handed over to various departments within Land Rover which either would be or had already been involved with Jay. Some became the subjects of the first publicity photographs of the new Discovery.

. . . and a name
One of the last tasks was to find a name for the new vehicle. The Jay Team started with 842 possibilities, which were gradually whittled

The Discovery bodyshell had a steel inner skeleton, similar in principle to the Range Rover's. Here it is before the steel roof has been welded in place . . .

. . . and here it is with the roof, but before the aluminium alloy skin panels have been added. Note the clever design, which made for minimal changes between three-door and five-door variants.

down to a short list of 15, and these were tested out at customer clinics. Some particularly good ones were put aside for possible use on future

Discovery is the name for a £45 million bargain

products, but the final choice of Discovery was a clear favourite – even though it was already in use as the code-name for the new Range Rover project (which was renamed Pegasus in 1989 as a result). Not the least important elements in its appeal were that it was easy to pronounce in all languages and already carried its own familiarity and image worldwide because of the space discovery programme.

The launch

The Land Rover Discovery was announced at the Frankfurt motor show on Tuesday, September 12, 1989, the choice of a major continental European show reflecting Land Rover's marketing intentions. The project had pioneered new methods of working, had taken just over two and a half years and had cost only £45 million. It was an extraordinary achievement in motor industry terms, all the more so because the vehicle went on to become such an overwhelming success. Land Rover managers were themselves quite flabbergasted by what the company had achieved, and one anecdote sums up their amazement perfectly. Commercial Director Chris Woodwark had the job of introducing the Discovery to the press at Frankfurt, and when preparing his speech he began to wonder whether anybody would believe how little the Discovery had cost to develop. So he added £100 million to the real figure when he gave that speech. The assembled press and industry still thought the Discovery had been a bargain!

The Jay Project team with the vehicle they created. Project leader Mike Donovan is on the far right of the picture, standing in the front row.

CHAPTER 3

BECOMING ESTABLISHED

Discovery, 1989-1991

Although both three-door and five-door bodies had been planned right from the beginning of Project Jay, only the three-door was announced at Frankfurt in September 1989, and Land Rover refused to comment on the possibility of a five-door model at a later date. Of course, one reason why the five-door was held over was to spread the capital cost of new tooling, but the main reason was that Discovery had to appear as different as possible from the Range Rover, which by this stage was sold predominantly as a four-door model. In addition, Land Rover believed that the vehicle's success depended on the creation of a trendy, 'lifestyle' image – which was best achieved through the three-door model.

The need to distinguish Discovery from its Range Rover parent also explained why these first examples had a 144bhp carburetted 3.5-litre petrol engine while the Range Rover switched to a 185bhp injected 3.9-litre type, and why no automatic transmission was available. These were purely marketing ploys, but they worked. The predominance in sales of the new 111bhp 200Tdi diesel engine did the rest, and most potential buyers perceived Discovery as a completely separate model from the Range Rover. The motor trade saw things rather differently, however, and when the first secondhand Discoverys hit the market a few months after the launch they were often described in advertisements as Range Rover Discoverys!

These first Discoverys all came with Sonar Blue interior trim, which was certainly distinctive but hardly sophisticated, and with the garish side stripes which had been inspired by similar decal treatments on Japanese vehicles sold in Europe. There were no alloy wheels at first, and although Land Rover Parts put some five-spoke items onto the market as soon as it could, these could not be ordered as a line-fitted option.

This of course was part of the marketing strategy associated with the Discovery. The bargain-basement price for the basic vehicle of £15,750 for either V8 or Tdi versions in the UK looked extremely attractive, but it was usually heavily inflated by a number of line-build options (listed below) and by various accessories from Land Rover Parts. In the words of the 1989 press release, these included 'items designed to protect the exterior and interior of the vehicle plus external utility accessories such as sports equipment carriers, sporting wheels, lighting, winching and towing accessories. In addition there are high-tech items such as cellular telephones which are compatible with fax and data communication machines and a compact disc player featuring multi disc selection.'

That marketing strategy went much further than anything Land Rover had done before. Following in the footsteps of a number of European luxury car manufacturers, Land Rover had decided to foster brand awareness and brand loyalty (as well as making a little extra money) by having Land Rover Parts sell a whole range of leisurewear and gifts bearing the Discovery logo. These ranged from straightforward items like a key ring, through roller-ball pens, sports holdalls, ski jackets and beach towels, to a picnic basket and an umbrella. They were aimed, said the press release, 'at the active family'. It was all a far cry from the workhorse market where the Ninety and One Ten sold, and from the rather more rarefied luxury market where the Range Rover sold. In due course, however, Land Rover Parts would expand its selection of non-vehicular accessories to cover Land Rover's other two model-ranges as well.

The first press picture of the Discovery was issued on July 7, 1989, and showed the side profile only. The vehicle would not be unveiled until the Frankfurt show, four months later.

Even Land Rover's dealerships had invested heavily in the new vehicle, which of course represented a bright new future for them as well as for the parent company. As Rover Group Managing Director George Simpson told journalists at a briefing just a few hours before the Discovery was unveiled at Frankfurt in 1989: 'Over the past two years, our dealers in the United Kingdom and overseas have been

First impressions from a test drive on Dartmoor

preparing for the new model. In the UK alone, the 130 Land Rover dealers have been investing heavily in new showrooms and workshops in anticipation of Discovery. We know that they have invested over £100 million as part of their plans to improve their own businesses with the introduction of a third product line-up.'

Test drives
One or two motoring journalists had a chance to drive the new Discovery before it was even seen in public, but the majority had to wait until October, when Land Rover organized a major ride-and-drive exercise on Dartmoor. *Land Rover Owner* editor Richard Thomas was there, and he was hugely impressed by the vehicle: 'I am thrilled by the Discovery and I'm really looking forward to seeing them in their thousands on the roads of Europe,' he wrote in the magazine's December 1989 issue. 'I am also very pleased for the people who work at Land Rover; they've done us proud.

'It's a real pleasure to see a British company designing, creating and building a world-beating vehicle. Land Rover has done it twice before with the original Land Rover and then the Range Rover, by luck more than judgment, probably. This time luck has played no part – the Discovery is pure judgment.

'And unless my judgment is totally shot away, Discovery is set for a meteoric rise to stardom and a long, well deserved reign at the top of the 4x4 pack.'

The fact was that the use of the Range Rover chassis had contributed to the first-rate ride and to handling which was exemplary by 4x4 standards of the time. In truth, the steering was rather vague, and the body rolled

This early left-hand-drive model is one of the batch registered with G...WAC numbers and used as press demonstrators, publicity vehicles and for engineering development. It is a V8 model (note the decal on the wing) without the optional twin sunroofs.

The stepped lower edge of the tail door window is very clear in this picture of an early Tdi model. The single exhaust outlet identifies the engine in this one, which was photographed before it received the standard Tdi decals on wings and tail door.

disconcertingly in corners taken energetically. Nevertheless, it was all just about acceptable, and the shortcomings were largely masked by the vehicle's many other positive features. These included the high-up driving position – which Land Rover later took to calling the 'command' driving position – the perceived strength and therefore crashworthiness of the Discovery, the spacious interior and, to a large extent, its fashionable appeal. The V8 gave excellent performance, being quiet and powerful, and the excellent fuel economy and strong pulling

power of the Tdi engine tended to make buyers forget that it was actually quite a rough and noisy engine.

Of course, the Discovery was aimed at a whole cross-section of the public. Its off-road ability, towing ability and ruggedness inevitably appealed to traditional Land Rover buyers; its comfort, performance and versatility made it a good Range Rover substitute for those who could not quite aspire to Solihull's finest; but perhaps the largest percentage of potential buyers were a new breed of Land Rover customer, for whom the Discovery would represent a first move into four-wheel drive.

'I suspect,' wrote Richard Thomas, 'buyers of Discovery will rarely, if ever, consider using the vehicle's off-road capabilities to the full.' How right he was: many of the people who bought Discoverys rarely tackled conditions more challenging than the hypermarket car park or the school run, and quite a high proportion of them never bothered to find out what that stubby little lever in front of the gear-lever was for! Land Rover, of course, laughed all the way to the bank as sales quickly exceeded even the company's best predictions.

The options

The early Discoverys were really quite basic vehicles by comparison with the later models because almost everything which could be considered non-essential was offered as an extra-cost option. In its most basic form, the Discovery could boast of power-assisted steering, but it did not have electric windows, central door locking, or a sunroof, and its rear loadspace was exposed to the prying eyes of all and sundry.

Conventional solid paint was standard – with the decals of course – and black, metallic and micatallic paints cost extra. A radio was fitted for most markets, but the high-specification set, with remote controls for volume and station search fitted around the edge of the instrument binnacle, was another extra-cost option. Rear mudflaps were standard but front ones cost extra, and the fixed roof rails and removable crossbars which made up the roof rack were also an option. Twin sun hatches – one above the front seats and one above the rear – cost extra, and there were storage bins at each side of the load area unless the buyer ordered the inward-facing foldaway seats which made the vehicle a seven-seater. It was no surprise that a towing pack was not standard, or that air conditioning cost extra. However, the so-called 'low emission' exhaust system, which incorporated a catalytic converter and was standard with the V8 engine on German-market models, was only available elsewhere to special order and inevitably brought a reduction in power.

Other options were marketed in groups or 'packs', which had the benefit of simplifying assembly on the lines at Solihull. Thus, the Electrical Pack consisted of electric front window lifts, central door locking, electrically-adjusted door mirrors with de-icer elements, and a headlamp power wash. The Security Pack

The dashboard was refreshingly different, although it seems quite dated now. Just visible in the foreground is the optional shoulder bag, attached to the centre console and matching the upholstery. The author still uses one as a camera case!

Twin removable glass sunroofs were an option, but the roof nets above the rear seat were standard. Note also the map pockets above the sun-visors.

This picture of the interior shows the light and airy feel provided by the large glass area, Alpine lights and optional sunroofs. The seats are fitted with washable protectors, one of many accessories available from Land Rover Parts.

The seven-seat option provided two inward-facing occasional seats in the rear. These folded into the sides of the load bay when not in use. Note the lap belts and the large zipped bag on the back of the rear bench seat – designed for stowage of the removable sunroofs.

Accessories again: the rear ladder provided access to the optional roof rack, designed for heavier-duty use than the roof bars over the front seats. The rear step retracted hydraulically when not in use. Only the 1990-model V8s had this type of twin-tailpipe exhaust; the 1991 and later V8i types had a single tailpipe outlet.

had a removable roller-blind loadspace cover and a detachable shoulder bag, which fitted to the rear of the console when not in use. And in Britain, there was a Special Value Pack, which combined the Electrical and Security Packs with the roof rack and twin sun hatches, for a discount on the total price of these items if ordered separately.

Production and sales

The Discovery did not go on sale in all of Land Rover's markets at once because production volumes took time to build up and the target of 300 vehicles a week was not attained until the end of 1989. There was a pause after the Frankfurt show announcement while stocks of the new vehicle built up, and then it went on sale for the first time on November 16 in Britain and Italy. After a further pause, sales began over the first few months of 1990 in France, Spain, Belgium, Holland, Germany, Switzerland, Austria, Finland and Norway. Africa and the Middle East were not on the agenda in those early days, and nor was the USA, where Land Rover's strategy since re-entering the market in 1987 had been to establish itself as a premium brand by selling only the high-priced Range Rover.

In Britain, sales of 1,533 vehicles in the three months from January to March 1990 made the Discovery the best-seller in its class with a margin of nearly 500 vehicles over its nearest competitor. When the six-month figures were announced in July, 3,173 UK sales between January and June had increased the Discovery's lead and were almost double the sales of its nearest rival. Meanwhile, during those six months a further 4,954 Discoverys were sold in continental Europe, the three best returns being from Italy (1,879 vehicles), France (1,148) and Spain (929).

Diesels prove the favourite as five-door arrives

Land Rover had been absolutely right to put so much effort into developing a class-leading diesel engine. Some European countries were taking only diesel models, and those 3,173 sales in Britain broke down into 2,438 diesels and just 735 petrol models. In other words, despite the excellent track record of the V8 engine, the diesel Discovery was being bought by three out of every four customers in a country where diesel power was still widely considered to be unacceptable in an everyday car!

Five doors and fuel injection

The Land Rover people listened carefully to customer feedback during the first 12 months of

The Gemini engine, known as the 200Tdi for public consumption, quickly proved the more popular of the two options available at the Discovery's launch. The position of the brake servo makes clear that this is a left-hand-drive vehicle.

Another left-hand-drive vehicle, this time with the carburettor version of the 3.5-litre V8 engine, which would be available for just a year.

Discovery sales, but it was pretty clear that they had got the vehicle right. There were niggles, of course, such as weak hinges on the big rear door, but there were no fundamental problems to be tackled. So the strategy which the company had planned for the vehicle went ahead without a hitch, and the 1990 motor show saw some important revisions to the range.

The big news was that the five-door body became available as an alternative to the three-door. While the three-door with its attention-grabbing side graphics had done an excellent job in establishing the Discovery's image in the market place, it had also helped to build up demand for a rather more sober vehicle which

Fuel-injected V8 provides more urge and economy

might suit the family buyer. The five-door Discovery was just such a vehicle.

The only graphics on the side were small 'Discovery' logos just behind the front wheelarches, and the two inward-facing rear seats came as standard equipment. In addition, the standard five-door specification included electric windows, central locking, headlamp washers, power-adjustable door mirrors with demister elements, a loadspace roller-blind and unique five-spoke alloy wheels. As before, Land Rover Parts could oblige with a collection of

extra-cost accessories, including side decals for those who really wanted them.

Meanwhile, a number of revisions affected both three-door and five-door models. The V8 petrol models were now renamed V8i and came with a 163bhp injected version of the 3.5-litre engine, which offered both greater performance and better fuel economy than the original carburettor engine. For the environmentally conscious, it was possible to order an exhaust catalyst at extra cost, when engine power dropped to 153bhp and a 'catalyst' decal was added to the rear door. Such models took the Discovery into Middle Eastern markets from September 1990. Five extra paint colours became available, plus one substitution, which took the total to 14, and instead of the rather startling Sonar Blue interior, customers could now ask for the much more restrained Bahama Beige alternative.

Inevitably, experience of the Discovery in service had suggested a few minor changes. The five-spoke alloy wheels formerly available only through Land Rover Parts could now be had as a line-fitted option on three-door models, and air conditioning was no longer exclusive to V8-powered models. A new grab handle on the E-post came as part of the seven-seater package and there were better stowage arrangements for the belts of the inward-facing seats. The edge of the rear door now had a red warning light and reflector to improve safety in poor light conditions, and there was an intermittent wiper setting for the rear window. Flush-fitting lower anchorages for the rear seat belts removed a source of annoyance when stowing bulky loads, and a pair of additional bass speakers were fitted in the front doors when the optional high-specification audio system was ordered. There

The five-door version appeared for 1991. Side graphics were conspicuous by their absence in most markets, and there was just a small Discovery logo on each front wing. Note the V8i wing badge – for 1991 brought the injected engine – and the chunky-looking five-spoke wheels, which were unique to the five-door in most countries. The roof rails were optional on three-doors, but standard on five-door models.

The interior was much the same as in the three-door models, but the extra doors made for a much more practical family vehicle.

The injected version of the 3.5-litre V8 brought a power increase of 19bhp in non-catalysed form, or 9bhp when equipped with an exhaust catalyst.

Side demister vents were added to the outer ends of the facia on 1991 models.

were also side demister vents at each end of the facia to maintain visibility of the door mirrors through the window glass.

Great success

The five-door Discovery proved an instant hit with the buying public, for whom it offered a real alternative to a mundane family estate car.

A credible alternative to a conventional car

While it most certainly ate into sales of the three-door model, it also firmly established the Discovery in the most lucrative sector of the market – which, of course, had been Land Rover's intention right from the beginning.

Yet the five-door model also helped to bring about a further shift in Land Rover's position as a manufacturer of 4x4 vehicles. In order to attract new buyers, the Discovery had to be a credible alternative to a conventional car, so it had to offer a number of features expected in a car in addition to all the features expected in a Land Rover product. The Range Rover had initiated the process when it had been upgraded to compete with top-quality saloons in the luxury market; the County Station Wagons had already started to blur the distinction between workhorse Land Rover and car substitute; and the Discovery would now take all this one stage further.

So the Discovery helped to bring about a fundamental change in Land Rover's market image and in the perceptions the company had of itself. What had been simply a specialist vehicle manufacturer was about to step into the mainstream as a fully-competitive car manufacturer without losing any of the credibility it had built up in the specialist 4x4 field over the years. It was a major step – but Land Rover proved able to pull it off.

CHAPTER 4

BROADER HORIZONS

From 1991 to 1996

The Discovery went from strength to strength in the early Nineties. Sales continued to increase and Land Rover kept on raising production to keep up with demand. During the first season of the five-door variant's availability (the 1991 model-year, which ran from September 1990 to August 1991), Discovery production at Solihull had been running at 500 vehicles a week – substantially more than the 300 a week which had been the target less than a year earlier. From August 1992 it went up by 10 per cent to 550 a week, and later in the season by a further 27 per cent to 700 a week to cope with demand. Even this was not enough, and as the 1994 model-year was about to open in August 1993, Land Rover announced that production would be increased by another 28 per cent to 900 vehicles a week. The sky seemed to be the limit.

After the initial launch in Europe, Land Rover had continued to introduce the Discovery into new markets, and demand from these was one reason for the production increases. The 1992 model-year, for example, saw the vehicle introduced into Japan, Australia, South Africa and a number of Middle Eastern countries, and Land Rover claimed that more than 70 per cent of all Discoverys made were now going for export. Another reason for the increased demand was that several new variants were introduced during this period, so by the end of the 1994 model-year the Discovery was available with two different body styles and three different engines, of which one could be ordered optionally with automatic transmission. A number of special variants were also offered by the Special Vehicle Operations division (later renamed Land Rover Special Vehicles), amongst which the Police Discovery was proving a huge success in Britain, where it was slowly but surely supplanting the Range Rover as a highly versatile motorway patrol vehicle.

The 1992 models
The Discovery model for 1992 was announced to the press in August 1991 and was first seen in public at motor shows in September. Five-door models were easy to distinguish from 1991 models because they had a rubbing strip down each flank, while the three-doors had new side graphics incorporating a 'compass' design.

The five-door specification was also upgraded slightly, the earlier Security Pack of the centre console's detachable shoulder bag and the roller-blind loadspace cover becoming standard equipment. All models also benefited from a redeveloped version of the five-speed gearbox known as the LT77S, which had modified synchromesh on first and second gears to give smoother selection. This change was long overdue: the difficulty of selecting second gear when cold had been a feature of the original LT77 gearbox ever since its appearance in the mid-Seventies on the Rover 3500 and Triumph TR7!

There were minor equipment variations on the basic Discovery models for different markets. Some overseas markets, for example, wanted side graphics on the five-door models, whereas in Britain the five-door models normally had unadorned sides because the family buyers who mostly bought them wanted something a little more discreet. In Switzerland, the importers saw a niche for something special and in September 1991 announced the Discovery Country Life limited edition, which was based on a five-door, five-speed V8i model with metallic paint and air condtioning. There were just 50 of these, which had leather upholstery and a leather-bound Nardi steering wheel, wood trim on the doors, facia and

The anti-roll bars and low-profile tyres of the Freestyle Choice package came with a new design of five-spoke alloy wheel, seen here on an early five-door Mpi model.

console, a picnic hamper and special decal badging. Most buyers had to make do with something rather less exclusive, of course, and the wide range of accessories marketed through Land Rover Parts certainly allowed any Discovery to be personalized to quite a high degree.

In Britain, changes in the Car Tax laws introduced in the April 1992 budget led to the creation of a new variant and to the renaming of the existing five-door models as the Tdi S and V8i S – although neither of them ever wore 'S' badges. In order to be able to offer a five-door Discovery at a price below the new £20,000 company car tax threshold, Land Rover deleted a number of items from the standard specification to produce a turbodiesel model known simply as the Discovery Tdi five-door. This lacked the alloy wheels of the 'S' model, together with its sunroof, electric windows and inward-facing rear seats. It was available from May of that year.

The 1993 models
The major news for the 1993 model-year, which began in September 1992, was the arrival of the

Range Rover LSE with the air suspension which also became available on other Range Rover models. However, Land Rover continued to put considerable effort into the Discovery, and there were a number of changes for the new season.

The most important was the arrival of an automatic transmission option for the petrol-engined models. This was a four-speed German-made ZF type and was carried over from the Range Rover, where it had done sterling service since 1985. To maintain model differentials, however, the Discovery did not take on the Range Rover's chain-driven transfer box but retained its LT230 gear-driven type – which by now had been made quite acceptably quiet.

On the 1993 model-year Discoverys, a remote-control alarm-cum-immobilizer system was standardized, and roller-blinds also became standard on models fitted with a sunroof. There was now a choice of three in-car entertainment systems, and two new options were announced. The Freestyle Choice package consisted of attractive star-pattern five-spoke alloy wheels shod with 235/70 low-profile tyres, plus the anti-roll bars front and rear which had been

The 1992-model three-door Discoverys had new 'Compass' graphics on their flanks. This V8i model is wearing the optional alloy wheels with five flat spokes.

Rubbing-strips were added to the flanks of the 1992 five-door models.

Automatic transmission arrived as a 1993-season option on V8i models only.

introduced two years earlier on the Range Rover. This made a marked difference to the handling of the vehicle, eliminating much of the body roll so characteristic of the early models and thus making the Discovery even more readily acceptable as an alternative to a conventional family estate. Not surprisingly, it proved very popular, but the second new option seems to have been quite rare. This was a second air-conditioning system, which fitted to the rear of the centre console and supplied refrigerated and dehumidifed air to the rear passengers.

In France, Discovery sales were boosted at the end of the 1993 model-year by two special editions, introduced in June. The cheaper of these was the Freestyle, which was a metallic blue three-door or five-door with the Freestyle Choice wheel and suspension package, plus special decals. The more expensive was the County Rider, again available as a three-door or a five-door and finished in green with a coachline and special decals on the rear sides and bonnet. Designed to appeal to horse riders, this one came with an adjustable tow hitch,

floor mats, a PVC boot liner, wheelarch protectors and side rubbing strips, mudflaps, and a removable saddle rack in the load area.

A 90-degree twist for a 2-litre engine

A third engine – the 2-litre Mpi
Meanwhile, Land Rover had identified a number of countries where there was potential for selling a version of the Discovery with a smaller petrol engine. These were primarily countries where large petrol engines were heavily taxed (such as Italy, where it was prohibitively expensive to run a petrol vehicle with an engine

41

The T16 engine of the Mpi started life with a transverse installation in Rover cars and had to be turned through 90 degrees for the 'north-south' installation in the Discovery. Stamped into the cover above the Land Rover oval are the words 'Rover 16 valve'.

larger than 2 litres). So a new version was developed and brought to market in June 1993. This was known as the Mpi, those letters standing for the multi-point injection system fitted to its 1,994cc four-cylinder engine. Three-door, five-door and Mpi S five-door versions were offered in Britain, but the vehicle never sold well on the home market.

The engine pressed into service for the Discovery Mpi was the T16 type originally developed for Rover cars and available in the 820i saloon and 220GTi coupe. In the cars, this 16-valve engine was mounted transversely, so the Land Rover engineers had to re-orientate it in order to suit the north-south installation in the Discovery. Detuned slightly to give 134bhp, it seemed to fit neatly between the 111bhp of the 200Tdi turbodiesel engine and the 163bhp of the injected petrol V8. However, it was let down by its torque delivery: the maximum of 137lb.ft at 2,500rpm was only barely adequate for undemanding road motoring, and there was depressingly little torque lower down the rev range. The Discovery Mpi was disappointing off-road or as a towcar, but its top speed of 98mph helped it appeal to a certain type of buyer.

Interestingly enough, this small-engined Discovery had grown out of a development programme to produce a variant with very much better performance. In the early Nineties, Solihull's Product Planning Department had drawn up schemes for a Discovery with the turbocharged edition of the T16 engine which later went into the Rover Vitesse and the Rover 220 Turbo Coupe. 'I actually thought it would appeal considerably to the market. I thought it would have a sort of yuppie image; it might just have pulled over the sort of Golf GTi brigade!', remembers John Bilton, whose idea it was.

It is not clear which version of the turbocharged T16 engine was tried out in the single prototype built around 1991 (which was probably a gold-coloured five-door). Logic suggests that the 220 Turbo Coupe version would have been the better bet, however, because it developed its maximum torque of 175lb.ft at a useful 2,100rpm, whereas the peak torque of the Vitesse version was developed at 4,000rpm – not much use for a heavy off-roader. One way or another, it appears that this Discovery proved to be a real flyer: with 180bhp (Vitesse engine) or 197bhp (220 Turbo Coupe engine), its top speed would probably have been slightly higher than that of the existing V8 model!

However, the project was shelved when

42

With the introduction of the enlarged V8 engine in the short-lived 1994 models, the numbers '3.9' were cast into the plenum chamber cover, just as they had been on Range Rovers equipped with this engine.

Discovery sales continued to increase, although the work which had gone into it was not wasted. The basic engineering for the engine's installation had already been done, so when a need arose for a 2-litre Discovery, Land Rover simply revived the 2-litre Turbo project, removed the turbocharger, and took things from there. It appears that adding a turbocharger to an Mpi Discovery is not very difficult because the hardware already exists for the 800 Vitesse and 220 Turbo Coupe engines, and in Italy it is possible to buy just such a conversion through aftermarket specialists.

The 1994 model-year – a bigger V8

The 1994-model Discoverys were short-lived, being available only between September 1993 (when they were introduced at the Frankfurt motor show) and March 1994 (when they were replaced by the facelifted versions which Land Rover called 1995 models).

The most important change for the new season was to the V8i models, where the injected 3.5-litre petrol engine was replaced by the injected 3.9-litre type which had been fitted to the Range Rover since 1989. This came as standard with a catalytic converter, which had been only optional on the final 3.5-litre Discoverys, and put out 182bhp. This

represented an increase of about 12 per cent over the output of the injected 3.5-litre engine, and was some 16 per cent better than the more directly comparable catalyst-equipped version.

The new engine made almost no difference to the top speed of a manual Discovery, which remained at around 105mph, but it did ensure that the automatic model was very nearly as fast

3.9-litre V8 boosts torque and acceleration

as the older manual 3.5-litre, and it made a very great difference to acceleration times. Thus a 3.9-litre manual Discovery could reach 60mph from rest 3 seconds faster than a 3.5-litre manual, and would accelerate from 50mph to 70mph in fourth gear nearly 2 seconds faster. Off-road performance was undiminished and potentially even better, as the 3.9-litre engine brought a massive torque increase over the 3.5-

43

From June 1993 the three engine options for the Discovery were revealed by tailgate badging. When the V8i was fitted with a catalytic converter in the exhaust, an additional 'Catalyst' decal was added beside the engine designation.

Different markets demanded different cosmetics. This '3.9 V8' was applied to the 1994-season Australian V8i models. *(Picture by courtesy of Patrick Sutcliffe.)*

litre type.

At the same time as the 3.9-litre engine arrived, all Discovery models took on a four-position electric headlamp levelling system (which had been available earlier in some export markets). The VIN was displayed on a small plate behind the windscreen as well as on the plate under the bonnet, as a theft deterrent measure, and an additional courtesy lamp was fitted in the E-pillar. When fitted, the optional CD player was now stowed under the passenger's seat. Asbestos-free brake pads were standardized and there were minor changes to the towing pack option. But that was all; Land Rover planned to save more major changes until the facelifted models arrived in March 1994.

The Honda Crossroad

Meanwhile, the success of the Discovery had not gone unnoticed by Honda, the Japanese company which had enjoyed a close working relationship with Land Rover's parent Rover Group since the early Eighties. There had never been any direct Honda input into the Land Rover side, mainly because the Japanese company had no off-road expertise to offer, although the majority of existing Rover-badged cars had been jointly developed with Honda.

Honda desperately wanted to offer a product in the booming 4x4 market, but their own CR-V was still some way off (and did not reach European markets until 1997). They therefore entered into a deal with Isuzu to market some of their off-roaders in the USA with Honda badges, and a second deal with Land Rover to market the Discovery with Honda badges in Japan. The deal allowed Land Rover to continue selling the Discovery with their own badges through Rover Group outlets in Japan. It represented an

important 'first', too: the first time a Japanese manufacturer had put its own badge on a foreign car for the Japanese market.

The agreement with Honda was announced in June 1993, and the first vehicles were shipped out to Japan for sales to begin in November. They were all five-door V8i models, and wore 'Honda Crossroad' badges. There were high hopes of big sales in Japan, not least because the vehicle would be sold through the 400-strong Verno dealer network, which was massively larger than the Rover Group network. However, the Crossroad never did achieve the 1,200 a year

---

Japanese prefer Land Rover to Honda badges

---

predicted, its best showing being in 1994 when 620 found buyers. Even the Japanese were not fooled by its Honda badges, and sales of the authentic Land Rover Discovery in Japan always exceeded those of the Crossroad by a big margin.

Discovery in Australia

The Discovery was also used to spearhead Land Rover's revival in Australia, where Toyota had long since taken over as the market-leader. The old Jaguar-Rover Australia (JRA) organization was wound up in April 1991 and replaced by a

Special decals were also applied to French Discoverys. Note the side shading on this 1992 model.

wholly-owned subsidiary of the Rover Group called Rover Australia, which more or less announced its arrival on the market by introducing the Discovery in May 1991.

The first Australian Discoverys were all three-door V8i types, with the low-compression, catalyst-equipped version of the engine to suit Australian emissions regulations and with air conditioning as standard to suit the local climate. For 1992, however, the range was broadened by the addition of five-door models in both V8i and Tdi forms. Air conditioning was a dealer-fit option on these, which nevertheless came as standard with what other markets knew as the Electrical Pack.

At the top of the 1992 Australian range was a model known and badged as the HL (for High Line), which came with air conditioning, alloy wheels, bumper-mounted driving lights, loadspace cover, shoulder bag, four ICE speakers and a coachline as standard. This could be based

on either a V8i or a Tdi five-door. Later in the year, a limited-edition Discovery Orienteer was announced, of which 75 were made. These were three-door V8i models with air conditioning, the five-spoke alloys from the five-door, 'compass' side graphics, driving lights, loadspace cover and shoulder bag. Each one also came with a special Orienteer compass keyring.

As the 1992 Orienteer edition sold out within six weeks, Rover Australia re-introduced it for 1993, alongside the new V8i five-door automatic model. Meanwhile, a huge new contract for exhaust catalysts signed between Land Rover and Johnson Matthey in Australia generated export credits, and the pound weakened against the Australian dollar. Rover Australia was able to drop Discovery prices and this, at a time when competitive Japanese models in Australia were becoming more expensive, gave the Land Rover product an even greater competitive edge over the opposition.

For Middle-Eastern markets there was an FXi model. These decals were used on all of them, but there were subtle differences between the vehicles supplied to locals and those to expatriate Britons. The locals demanded chromed bull-bars, side steps, etc whereas the expats preferred these items in black.

Having won *Overlander* magazine's 4WD of the Year award for two years running, the Discovery went on to boost Rover Australia's sales to such an extent that the company had become second only to BMW as a European car importer by the close of the 1993 season. For 1994, the company drew attention to the enlarged V8 engine by putting special red decal badges reading '3.9 V8' on the vehicles, and sales were even better.

CHAPTER 5

THE ROMULUS PROJECT

A facelift for 1995

The 1995 model-year Discovery was developed under the project code-name of Romulus, and the project was run in parallel with some major work on the Range Rover which was code-named Project Remus. Some of the powertrain changes associated with the Romulus and Remus projects also had an effect on the Defender, and the three revised models were introduced together. It is arguable that the Geneva motor show, which opened on March 4, 1994, was a little early to introduce the 1995 model-year vehicles, but that choice of date had been made partly to suit conditions in the US market, where the Discovery was to make its debut exactly one month later, on April 4.

In fact, the main thrust of the Romulus project had been to prepare the Discovery for the US market. However, just as on the 1987 Range Rover, several other upgrades were introduced at the same time and the complete package was designed to have worldwide appeal. The Romulus project was also designed to take the Discovery a little further upmarket by improving equipment levels and introducing a new flagship model. This was the first stage in the Discovery's move into the market segment hitherto occupied by the Range Rover, which itself would be entering a higher price bracket when the second-generation models arrived in September 1994.

The first public indication of what was in the wind came in a press release from Land Rover North America dated September 1993 in which company President Charles R Hughes was quoted as saying that when the Discovery was launched in the USA in April 1994 it would have dual airbags as standard. In fact it was shortly after that press release when the first examples of the US-specification Discovery came off the production lines. Eight of them would be shipped to Central America during January for the publicity exercise known as La Ruta Maya, the story of which is told in Chapter 7.

The Romulus changes were far more extensive than Hughes had hinted, however. The airbags – introduced ahead of forthcoming US legislation and seen on the Range Rover at the same time – were an important step in the sales battle because they made Land Rover the first manufacturer to offer such safety equipment on a 4x4. Other safety-related upgrades were part of the 1995 model-year package, and Romulus also took on the ABS which was available on the Range Rover, while

Discovery ES becomes the new flagship

the anti-roll bars, already optional on the Discovery, became a standard fitting. Refinement was improved in a number of areas, notably with a new manual gearbox and an improved turbodiesel engine, and of course there were both interior and exterior facelifts to make the new vehicles distinctively different from the old.

At the top of the range, selling at a price above any previous Discovery, was the new flagship model known as the Discovery ES. This was available with either the 3.9-litre petrol V8 or the revised 2.5-litre turbodiesel, but not with the 2-litre Mpi petrol engine. It came with either the familiar ZF four-speed automatic transmission or the new five-speed manual gearbox, and it incorporated as standard a number of features which were extra-cost options on lesser models. As for the name, a Land Rover spokesman at the time explained that the letters were chosen 'because we already have SE for the top-model Range Rover and we wanted this to be a bit different!' The new ES was not available in all markets, however, and was not sold in the USA – although it was possible to create an ES equivalent there by adding optional extras to the base vehicle. Meanwhile, in France, the 1995 models were badged as 'Discovery 2', and in Japan they continued to be available as badge-engineered Honda Crossroads.

Powertrain and chassis

Of the three engines available in earlier Discoverys, only the 3.9-litre V8 remained unchanged on the 1995 models. The 2-litre Mpi, criticized for its lack of bottom-end torque, had been modified to give a little more in that department – although the fact that its 140lb.ft were now developed at a high 3,600rpm made quite clear that this was still an engine for everyday road use, and not best suited to towing or off-road work. Land Rover made no publicity capital out of this change, but they did make a great deal of capital out of the major revisions to the best-selling turbodiesel engine. Both the Mpi and turbodiesel revisions, of course, were completely irrelevant for the US market, which would only receive V8 versions of the Discovery.

A great deal of work had gone into the Gemini engine since its launch in the Discovery in 1989. A year later, a detuned 107bhp version had become the standard powerplant for the utility models, newly renamed Land Rover Defenders. Then in 1992, the 200Tdi in 111bhp Discovery tune had replaced the 2.5-litre VM turbodiesel engine as the compression-ignition option for the Range Rover. By this time, work had already begun to produce trials vehicles for a large British Army contract, and a modified version of the engine known as Gemini 2 was used in some of these. Then new European regulations on diesel exhaust emissions were announced for 1996 introduction, and the Land Rover engineers decided to apply the changes necessary to meet these to the Gemini 2 engine. The result – introduced in the 1995 model-year Discovery, Range Rover and Defender at the same time – was known internally as the Gemini 3 engine. For public consumption, it was called the 300Tdi, the 3 coming from its Gemini 3 code-name and not, unfortunately, indicating a massive increase in maximum torque!

In fact, there was no increase in either torque or maximum power as compared to the original 200Tdi engine. Nor was there any change in the bore and stroke dimensions. The customers were quite happy with the existing performance of the engine, and Land Rover knew that to increase its cubic capacity would make it unsaleable in Italy – one of its best markets – where diesel engines larger than 2.5 litres were subject to punitive taxation. So all these elements of the original engine were retained unaltered, and the main thrust of the re-engineering work (emissions control apart) had been to tackle the complaints of noise and poor refinement, which had begun to surface after the novelty of the 200Tdi's excellence had worn off.

To these ends, no fewer than 208 components were changed, and among others the 300Tdi boasted a new cylinder head, fuel injectors, pistons, conrods, turbocharger, exhaust manifiold, timing belt, water pump and alternator. Perhaps most importantly for Land Rover, the redesigned engine also took less time

More refinement and a new manual gearbox

to build than its 200Tdi predecessor, thus reducing manufacturing costs. As far as the customers were concerned, however, the changes brought a huge increase in refinement. Although the engine was still a long way from being as quiet as the best indirect-injection types from other manufacturers, it was very much less obtrusive than the 200Tdi type, and it still offered the same outstanding economy which rival indirect-injection types could not match.

The new manual gearbox was called the R380 – R for Rover and the figure for the 380Nm (280lb.ft) of torque which was the limit of its capacity. It had been developed mainly to deal with criticism of the long-serving LT77S five-speed type as stiff and notchy, and Land Rover's aim had been to make a gearbox with a change as slick and easy as the best of its Japanese rivals. In this its engineers certainly succeeded, although the R380 gearbox suffered a number of warranty failures in its early days and for as long as three years after its introduction. The R380 also had a different gate pattern from the LT77S,

The Romulus project created the 1995-model Discovery, of which this is a five-door example. Most obvious in this picture is the restyled front end, but note also the blacked-out windscreen edges. The wheels are the five-spoke Freestyle Choice alloys.

From the rear the most obvious change was the addition of light clusters in the bumper. This is an ES model with some extras, including the large 'Discovery' decal on the lower body sides, and light guards. It is just possible to see that the rear lights under these guards no longer have amber indicator segments – a change which proved unpopular with customers.

a double-H with reverse behind fifth replacing the older type with reverse on a spur alongside first.

The revised turbodiesel engine and new gearbox were, of course, fitted to only a proportion of the new Discoverys, but the 1995 specification included some additional chassis refinements which affected the entire range. These were an acoustically decoupled rear propshaft (with a rubber doughnut to prevent noise being transmitted along the shaft) and rear spring isolators (to reduce noise transmission into the body). Crush cans at the front of the chassis also improved safety. These deformable canisters were designed to absorb the impact of a frontal collision and could be easily replaced, thus minimizing the need for expensive chassis repairs. On the Discovery, they were concealed behind the front bumper overriders.

The body
The exterior facelift for the Discovery was built around new and larger headlamps, which gave 20 per cent more illumination and allowed a redesign of the front end. The grille and indicator lamps were changed, along with the apron spoiler and bumper ends, and a bold 'Land Rover' decal on the leading edge of the bonnet completed the transformation, which made the vehicle look wider and more purposeful. That spoiler could also incorporate optional foglamps, which on earlier models had to be fitted in rather ugly add-on pods.

At the rear, the lights had also changed, although this time they had retained their shape and simply lost the amber indicator segment. Land Rover had been concerned about legislation which demanded that both rear lamps should be in full view of approaching traffic at all times, and had recognized that the right-hand lamp could be obscured if the tail door was open when the vehicle was stationary at night. So the lamps which might be in use – red tail markers and amber indicators – were incorporated in the bumper, and the indicators disappeared from the main light segments. Unfortunately, no-one had noticed that the left-hand bumper-mounted light would be obscured if the optional retractable rear step was fitted. A journalist pointed this out to Land Rover representatives during the pre-launch press

The redesigned interior featured restyled door trims.

The first Discoverys had Range Rover door mirrors, but a new design was drawn up for the Romulus vehicle.

event, and some hasty redesigning was set in train to get a suitable step ready for dealers to offer! The change to bumper-mounted indicators was not universally liked, either, and Land Rover soon reverted to the earlier type of main lamp cluster which incorporated the indicators, while retaining the new bumper-mounted lamps as an insurance policy.

Other external changes consisted of new side rubbing-strips, which had bright inserts on top

The high specification developed for the North American market spilled over onto mainstream models, which were now expanded to include an ES derivative with its own special badging.

models, bigger door mirrors and new Castor five-spoke alloy wheels with a central disc. ES variants had special decals and their wheels were a gunmetal-enamelled version of the Freestyle Choice five-spoke design. Sun hatches remained optional on some models and standard on others, and were now of the tilt-and-slide type, while electric operation was available at extra cost and standard on the ES. The exterior package was completed by a choice of four new colours.

The interior redesign focused on the new dashboard, with provision for airbags, although perhaps even more noticeable was that the trim had been toned down considerably from the earlier type. In particular, the original Sonar Blue colour had gone, to be replaced by Granite Grey as the alternative to Bahama Beige. There were fewer hard edges and concessions to fashion in the new Discovery interior, which retained all the practicality of its forebear, but was very obviously aimed much more at the family buyers who were by this time the main purchasers of Discoverys. The new option of leather seat trim, which was standard on the ES, bore witness to the move upmarket, and as before it was possible to order a CD player tucked away under the front passenger seat.

The dashboard was more curvaceous and integrated than before. Its centrepiece was a new heating and ventilation unit, which featured separate rotary controls for the driver and passenger in the current car idiom. The radio-cassette had also been repositioned higher up, which made it easier to operate, and there were pop-out cup holders in the centre to meet US market expectations. Switchgear, stalk controls and steering wheel were all new, too. The column stalks and steering wheel – whether with or without airbag – were one area where Land Rover had saved money in the Discovery facelift, however, as all of them came from the current Rover 800 saloon. Air conditioning for the rear passengers was optional, as before, although the bulky console-mounted unit had now been replaced by discreet aircraft-style nozzles in the headlining and a control switch between them.

Last but not least, there were several other less visible changes. These ranged from the side intrusion bars now incorporated in the front doors to meet US legislative requirements (but fitted to vehicles for all markets) to the courtesy light delay already seen on the Range Rover. In between came small items specially designed for the USA such as a warning chime which sounded if the driver's door was opened when the key was still in the ignition and a buzzer which sounded if the door was opened while the lights were on and the engine was switched off. There was also a new alarm system with volumetric and perimetric sensors, which was activated by the remote control used for the central locking, and the VIN was once again displayed on the facia, where it was visible through the windscreen as a further security measure.

Most important of the Romulus changes was the introduction of airbags, and both driver's and passenger's bags are fitted to the vehicle pictured here. The new rotary heater controls are clearly visible, as is the more sophisticated upholstery style which replaced the over-fashionable original.

New interior fabrics were developed to give the interior a more sophisticated air, although the characteristic head restraints were still in evidence.

Leather seats were available for the first time on a line-built Discovery, although they had been offered on the 1992-model Country Life limited edition in Switzerland.

The Romulus changes did not focus specifically on the Honda Crossroad version to be sold in Japan, but the vehicle adapted easily enough. This is a five-door V8i model.

The Tdi engine was thoroughly redeveloped to improve refinement and to meet forthcoming diesel emissions legislation in Europe. The new version was called the 300Tdi.

Big sales, big problems

The revised Discovery was extremely well-received in all markets, and at home in July 1994 it won the Best Off-Roader category in *Auto Express* magazine's New Car Honours. The worldwide success of the new models was also a major factor in making the 1994 calendar-year a record one for both Discovery and overall Land Rover production. But unfortunately Land Rover had to step up production yet again to cope with demand, and this led to the first signs of problems. Those associated with the R380 gearbox have already been mentioned, but the biggest problem was the fundamental one that the Discovery had not been designed to be built in such high volumes.

Production engineers in a modern car factory have their own input at the design stage, ensuring that the vehicle can be built without difficulty and can meet the desired quality standards. The Discovery had been production engineered for much lower volumes than those at which it was now being built, and it had been possible to make only a few changes as part of the 1995-season facelift. The result was a drop in standards of quality control – and both customers and the press began to complain loudly, particularly in view of the higher price now being asked and in view of the vehicle's now more elevated pretensions. The Discovery, ironically, had become a victim of its own success.

CHAPTER 6

MOVING ON UP

Discovery 1994-1998

Over the next four years, Land Rover's strategy was to continue moving the Discovery upmarket into the sector which was vacated by the original Range Rover (renamed the Classic in 1994) in 1996. This allowed two things to happen. First, it created a vacuum at the bottom end of the market into which the new Freelander would be moved when it was announced in 1997; and second, it allowed the new Range Rover to be moved ever higher up the price scale. There were variations on this strategy in different countries to suit the model-mix available there and local market conditions, but the basic strategy was followed worldwide.

The strategy is well illustrated by prices in the UK market. The Discovery was launched in 1989 with a base price of £15,750, and in 1997 the cheapest Freelander cost £15,995 – a striking similarity despite inflation over the intervening years. By the time the second-generation Discovery was introduced in 1994, its prices spanned the bracket from £17,640 to £25,765 and the Range Rover cost between £28,895 and £40,899. By April 1998, Discovery prices started at £21,270, thus leaving a vacuum below £20,000, and ran up to £31,490 – well into the territory once occupied by the Range Rover.

In order to justify this gradual increase in prices, Land Rover loaded the Discovery with more and more extra equipment. The move had really begun with the ES model in 1994, and between then and 1998 the Discovery took on many of the luxury and convenience features which had once been exclusive to the Range Rover, including a heated windscreen, wood interior trim, an automatic dipping mirror and power-adjustable front seats.

Discovery sales had seen an astonishing increase during the 1994 model-year, just prior to the introduction that March of the facelifted

versions which went on to take the US market by storm. Production hit new peaks, the best figures being those for the 1995 model-year, when Solihull cranked out no fewer than 69,919 examples of the Discovery.

However, figures began to slip after that. One reason was the increasing number of good secondhand Discoverys coming onto the market; another was that by this stage the Discovery was suffering from increasing competition, not least from the latest Jeep and Toyota products. News of the quality control problems, brought about primarily by the increased rate of production, must also have affected sales to some extent. For the 1996 model-year, Land Rover built 65,039 Discoverys, but for 1997 the figure was markedly down at 58,352. The 1998 totals had not been released at the time of writing, but it was clear by this stage that many customers were waiting for the third-generation Discovery scheduled for an autumn 1998 launch. In spite of falling sales, however, the Discovery was still generally viewed as the best vehicle in its class.

The 1995 models
As introduced in March 1994, the Discovery range in the UK consisted of three-door and five-door models, with Mpi, Tdi and V8i power options. Automatic transmission was optional on the Tdi and V8i, but not on the Mpi. The base-specification three-door and five-door models had steel wheels and five seats; next up were the unbadged five-door S models with alloy wheels, seven seats and certain other extras; and at the top of the range was the ES, available only as a five-door model with seven seats, twin airbags, ABS and air conditioning among its standard features. Airbags were an extra-cost option on all the other models, and it was

possible to order only a driver's-side bag rather than both. In Britain, as in most other countries, these were known as the 1995 models despite their early introduction; in the USA, however, as Chapter 7 explains, there would be further changes to create the 1995 models.

For most markets, however, there were no significant changes to the specification during the 1995 model-year. Nevertheless, the latest rear lamp arrangements were not univerally liked, and customer feedback prompted Land Rover to offer a kit with the old style of body-

The XS model brought a more sporty appearance to the Discovery range, with attractive deep-dish alloy wheels. This is a later, 1997 model.

In the 1998 model-year realignment, the mid-range model was designated Discovery GS. Note the gunmetal five-spoke alloys, formerly exclusive to the ES, the wing badge and the coachline.

mounted lamps and extra wiring as a dealer modification. By May 1995, new vehicles were being built with the old lamps as a matter of course, thus duplicating the indicator lamps still located in the rear bumper.

In Japan, the second-generation Discovery went on sale with 'Honda Crossroad' badges, but it was not a success and sold just 137 copies before being withdrawn. Customers preferred to buy the real thing, not least perhaps because its exclusivity was assured by the relatively small number of Land Rover dealerships in Japan. Rover Japan traded on this exclusivity, and in July 1995 introduced a Camel Trophy limited edition of 150 vehicles, each one carrying its own number on the tailgate. These models came as four-speed automatics with the 3.9-litre V8 petrol engine, or as five-speed manuals with the 300Tdi turbodiesel. All of them were painted in the correct Sandglow yellow and carried metal Camel Trophy event plates at each end of their full-size roof racks.

The 1996 models

Back in the UK, June 1995 was launch time for the freshened-up 1996 models. The main changes were the introduction of the XS model 'for customers seeking a more extrovert appearance for their vehicle' (as the press release put it), a power increase for the 300Tdi

in automatic models, and new Gleneden tweed-style seat fabric in Bahama Beige or Granite Grey. With the introduction of the XS, Discoverys in Britain came in four guises: the unnamed entry-level models, the unbadged S, the sporty XS and the luxurious ES.

The XS was an ABS-equipped seven-seater five-door petrol or turbodiesel, with bright paint colours, side rubbing-strips and wheelarch

Wheels lead the way to an extrovert image

protectors, special lower body graphics and some extremely attractive dished alloy wheels. These had been inspired by locally-sourced ones fitted to German Discoverys for some time, and they were fitted with 235/75 Goodyear Eagle tyres featuring raised white letters. This now complicated the wheel options available, and it is worth listing what was standard (at least in the UK) during the 1996 model-year.

Base models came with the same silver-painted styled steel wheels which had been fitted to Discoverys since 1989. The S model five-doors came with Castor alloy wheels as standard, featuring five flat spokes and a circular centre section; and optional on both base models and the S were the five-spoke Freestyle Choice wheels with a silver finish. The same wheels were given gunmetal-enamelled spokes and fitted to ES models under the name of Tornado wheels. Lastly, of course, the XS had unique deep-dish wheels with a silver finish.

The engine upgrade for the automatic turbodiesels was very welcome and reduced the

New EDC allows cruise control on turbodiesel models

acceleration times, which had been a source of some customer dissatisfaction. The 300Tdi was fitted with Electronic Diesel Control (EDC), which improved refinement and emission levels as well as boosting power by 8.4 per cent to 120bhp (90kw) and torque to 221lb.ft (300Nm). However, as a policy decision this version of the engine was not made available on manual models, no doubt because buyers of the automatic would again have complained about the performance discrepancy! The EDC equipment also enabled 1996-model Tdi automatics to be fitted with a cruise control, which had not been available on earlier turbodiesel Discoverys.

Other changes for 1996 were to the radio cassette and to the ES model, which gained eight-way power adjustment for its front seats. A robust engine immobilization system was also standardized across the range, and the remote-control handset which activated both this and the central locking was made smaller than the earlier type. Also, right at the end of the season, in summer 1996, a group of British dealers in the Midlands produced a special-edition five-door Discovery of their own. Known as the Discovery 150, this had special graphics, dished wheels and other items, and was visually similar to the XS. It was limited to 150 examples.

The 1997 models
The 1997 model-year brought no major changes except in the USA, as Chapter 7 explains. In Britain, sales were kept alive with the help of limited editions, although the first of these proved a minor embarrassment when its name was found to be a trademark belonging to someone else!

This first limited edition was announced at the London Motor Show in October under the name of Goodwood. There were to be 500 examples, all five-doors finished in metaliic British Racing Green (renamed as Goodwood Green for the occasion). The model had distinctive coachlines and unique badging, dished alloy wheels, beige Gleneden cloth upholstery, burr walnut interior trim, a leather-trimmed wheel and the top-class Traveller Audio Choice ICE system. Unfortunately, someone had forgotten to check whether there might be any problem with using the Goodwood name. There was: the owners of the racing circuit objected that it was their trademark, so the show vehicle remained the only one badged as a Goodwood, the remaining 499 vehicles simply going out as an unnamed limited edition.

Nevertheless, this limited edition kept sales ticking over and at the turn of the year Land Rover gave their approval to an even more exclusive limited edition, this time prepared by Lex Land Rover, of Maidenhead, in conjunction with *Horse and Hound* magazine. Announced in January 1997, there were just 20 Horse and Hound models, based on the five-door Tdi S with certain optional items standardized. They also had special decals on the wings and a limited-edition number on the facia, and came with several promotional items of interest to

Limited editions and optional body styling kits

horse owners – including a year's subscription to the magazine.

Factory-produced limited editions continued with the Argyll, announced in June 1997. The 600 five-door Argylls were based on V8i S or Tdi S models, finished in Oxford Blue or new Woodcote Green paint, with dished alloy wheels and appropriate badging. Like the limited edition originally named the Goodwood, the Argyll could be bought with either the Tdi or the V8 engine; in either case, automatic transmission was available, but the manual gearbox could be ordered only with the turbodiesel engine. This reflected customer

Very different decor was used for some overseas markets. This five-door was destined for Angola in 1996.

demand at the time: there was little call for the Mpi engine, or for the manual gearbox in the V8i models.

Meanwhile, December 1996 had seen the introduction of an optional body styling kit for five-door Discoverys. Known as Bodystyle Choice and designed by Ian Callum, the man responsible for Aston Martin's DB7, it was moulded from a resilient material called R-RIM. The core kit consisted of a front apron with circular foglamp lenses, integrated bodyside mouldings and wheelarch protectors, bumper end caps and a rear apron. To these could be added a second kit of new sills, and a third consisting of a rear roof spoiler. The items were available either painted to match the vehicle's body or in their natural gunmetal grey finish. In Britain, however, they were not popular, so they were never used on a limited-edition model.

1998: new names

New model names characterized the 1998-model Discoverys. Positioned just above the base models in the UK were new three-door XS variants, which joined the existing XS five-

doors. The best-selling S models were renamed GS types and the ES remained at the top of the range. All these models were available with either the 300Tdi or the 3.9-litre V8 engine, but the slow-selling Mpi models disappeared altogether. Manual and automatic transmissions remained available with both the 1998-season engines.

All models now had front mudflaps as standard and came with the third high-mounted stop lamp introduced earlier on US models. New rear-lamp clusters met the latest regulations, and headlamp levelling and electric front windows were now standard across the range. Five-doors could have a heated windscreen at extra cost, and there were six new paint colours, all applied using the latest water-borne paint technology. GS models had two manual sunroofs and roof rails as standard, and the ES had a walnut facia rail and heater control surround panel.

There were interior changes for 1998, too. Gleneden fabric gave way to Kestrel cloth in grey or beige, and models with leather or part-leather seats gained a rear centre armrest. On

This Argyll five-door limited edition of summer 1997 was followed in 1998 by a three-door version.

the top-model ES it was possible to order a Premium Trim Pack consisting of Lightstone Beige leather with Bahama Beige piping, plus stainless steel door sill plates. With the Premium trim came 'Premium' badges attached to wings and tailgate.

The choice of wheels changed again. Styled steel wheels remained standard on the entry-level models, while Castor alloys became the Freestyle option on three-doors and the deep-dish wheels the Freestyle option on five-doors. The XS took on new wheels known as Sculptured Silver Alloy types, and a gunmetal-finish version of these was used on the ES. The GS, meanwhile, came with the Tornado gunmetal-finish five-spokes formerly used on

the ES. That, at least, was the UK line-up; in other countries, there were variations to suit local market conditions.

The UK also had a new limited edition, based on the seven-seater GS model. This was called the Aviemore and was designed around a winter sports theme. It came with dished alloy wheels and a heated windscreen, and was available only in British Racing Green with beige cloth upholstery or Rioja Red with grey cloth upholstery. As usual, there were special badges. Then in April 1998, the Argyll name used on the 1997 limited edition returned on a regular-production three-door model positioned between the base model three-door and the XS version.

The final special edition for the UK was the Discovery Safari, introduced in June 1998.

The Discovery Anniversary 50 celebrated Land Rover's 50th anniversary as a marque. Note the Boost alloy wheels, which were not available on any other UK model, and the '50th Anniversary' badge on the front wing.

The final special editions

That was not all: the Aviemore and the Argyll were followed by two more special editions during June 1998. The first of these was called the Discovery Anniversary 50 and the second the Discovery Safari – which would be the last of the limited editions based on the second-generation

Anniversary 50 to mark a Land Rover milestone

models. By this time, sales of the Discovery were flagging badly in Britain, partly under the impact of Freelander sales (which had begun in January 1998) and partly because buyers were waiting for the new Discovery, which the motoring media had told them would be announced in the autumn.

Nevertheless, the Discovery Anniversary 50

was not designed solely to boost flagging sales. Land Rover celebrated its 50th anniversary as a marque during 1998, and in Britain the company introduced Collectors' Edition variants of all four model ranges. The Anniversary 50 was the Discovery version, and it was announced on June 5, 1998.

Like the limited-edition Range Rover Vogue 50, Defender V8 50 and Freelander 50th, the Discovery Anniversary 50 was specially finished in Atlantis Blue metallic paint. However, White Gold was optional, and with either colour there were 50th Anniversary logo badges on each front wing and on the tailgate. The model was specifically marketed as a limited edition, and Land Rover UK Managing Director Peter Kinnaird promised that it would be made available only in very low numbers. Exactly how many were to be built was not disclosed, however: Land Rover wanted to gauge the demand first.

The Anniversary 50 came as a Tdi manual, a Tdi automatic, or a V8i automatic. It had Lightstone leather upholstery as standard, and a number of other items mainly or uniquely associated with the North American models. These were Boost alloy wheels with 235/70 x 16 tyres, polished stainless steel kickplates, an

In July 1996 a group of UK dealers got together to create the limited-edition Discovery 150, which had some visual similarities to the XS.

There was one Discovery Goodwood – the 1996 motor show car. The name was found to be someone else's trademark and was deleted from the rest of the limited edition.

automatic dimming rear-view mirror and a heated windscreen. Also in the specification were air conditioning, the seven-seat configuration, roof bars, a CD changer, front foglamps, a leather-rimmed airbag steering wheel, and a bright insert in the side rubbing strip. Strangely, however, a passenger's-side airbag was still an optional extra.

The Safari limited edition followed on June 22. It consisted of 1,100 vehicles based on the five-door, seven-seat GS model, and came in Epsom Green with air conditioning, twin sunroofs, Tornado alloy wheels, a driver's airbag, heated windscreen and CD player. Distinguishing external features included a 'soft' A-frame bar carrying foglamps, a rear door-mounted ladder, roof rails and chrome-finish running-boards. Like the 50th Anniversary edition, it was available as a Tdi with manual or automatic transmission, or as a V8i with automatic transmission only.

European limited editions

Britain was not alone in creating these limited editions, of course. In the Netherlands, for example, there was a five-door Discovery Trophy, and in Germany – where the Discovery was selling strongly – there was a Sunseeker special

edition during 1996, while the 1998 season saw no fewer than three special editions.

The 1996 Sunseeker five-door model came in metallic blue with special decals, with deep-dish alloy wheels like those on the XS, and with a chromed A-bar of the type favoured in Germany. The 1998 Camel Trophy edition came as a three-door or five-door, in correct Sandglow paint,

Limited-edition models in the overseas markets

with Tornado alloy wheels and 235/70 x 16 tyres. Extra equipment included a bull-bar, a raised air intake and a roof rack with ladders and additional spotlamps. Air conditioning was available at extra cost. Confusingly, there was also a Trophy edition, only available with the 300Tdi engine. This had Tornado alloy wheels, twin airbags, air conditioning, metallic paint, a

Limited editions were distinguished by special badges. This is the Aviemore.

The Premium trim option on the ES model for 1998 also brought special badging, seen here.

Just 20 Horse and Hound Discoverys were built in 1997, making this special edition rare and exclusive.

chromed A-bar with long-range driving lamps, and a special spare wheel cover. Even more exclusive – and expensive – was the Discovery Esquire, available in either Tdi or V8i guise. Twin airbags and air conditioning were allied to ABS, a leather-and-wood interior, alloy wheels, metallic paint and standard foglamps.

Discovery in Australia
Australia had for many years been one of Land Rover's most successful overseas markets, and for that reason the introduction of the 1995-

model Discovery was an important event in that country. Both V8i and Tdi models were offered, but there was no Mpi, and automatic transmission was optional on all models except the three-door Tdi. Top of the range was the ES, with twin airbags and alloy wheels as standard, but these items cost extra on every other model. The Australian second-generation Discoverys came with air conditioning as standard and with a centre high-mounted stop lamp like that on US-market vehicles.

However, Rover Australia did not do as well

Australian Discoverys had their own model hierarchy and badging in 1997, as this picture shows.

with the 1995 Discovery as they had hoped. One reason was the entry of Jeep to the Australian market with strongly competitive products, and another was the restricted supply of vehicles available from Solihull. So the company resolved to raise the profile of the Discovery just before the start of the new model-year with a limited-edition model known as the Rossignol. Named after the makers of ski equipment and fitted out for a weekend on the ski slopes, the Discovery Rossignol was produced in just 100 examples. Basically a three-door V8i, the Rossignol had Caprice blue-green metallic paint like that used on the 1993 UK-market Defender 90SV. It also had a ski-rack on the roof, side rubbing-strips and wheelarch protectors, special side stripes, driving lamps and a number of other items from the options list.

By October 1995, Rover Australia knew that they wanted a strong entry-level model, which they were already describing as the Discovery S.

However, worldwide demand for the Discovery was by then putting such pressure on Land Rover's production lines that it was February 1997 before the Australian range was realigned. It followed the North American pattern of a three-tier range, the entry-level model being the S, the mid-range model the SE and the top model the SE7. All carried appropriate decal badging on the front wings and tailgate, and Rover Australia were rewarded with the improved sales they had wanted – although much later than would have been ideal.

This model range lasted just a year, and was replaced by a four-model range in February 1998. The S, SE and SE7 types remained, although they were no longer badged as such. The fourth model was a new top-of-the-range type called the LS, available only with the V8 engine and automatic transmission, and in other respects broadly similar to the ES sold in other countries.

CHAPTER 7

ACROSS THE ATLANTIC

Discovery in North America, 1994-1998

Land Rover had a chequered history in the USA and Canada until the late 1980s. Exports began in late 1949, when the Rover Company did a deal with Rootes Motors Inc (the North American arm of the British Rootes Group) to arrange distribution. Nevertheless, sales were slow – desperately so in the USA, though the Canadians had more sympathy for the British-built vehicle.

Rover established its own subsidiary in 1958 under the name of the Rover Company of North America. Its headquarters were initially in Toronto, with a branch office in New York, but from 1960 New York became the head office and Toronto the branch. Sales improved under new management in the 1960s, but were still not great. Nevertheless, the Rover Company persevered and considered it worthwhile to develop special versions of their four-wheel drives to meet new US legislation in 1968. Yet sales were simply not enough, and Land Rover withdrew from the US and Canadian markets in summer 1974 when further investment would have been needed to meet increasingly strict exhaust emissions controls.

Private imports apart, Land Rover did not figure in the USA or Canada again for 12 years. As Chapter 1 makes clear, Tony Gilroy's plan for rescuing the company involved re-entering the North American market, and by 1987 the Range Rover had been redeveloped to spearhead this new assault. Introduced in March that year and sold by a company named Range Rover of North America (to avoid confusing buyers), it proved every bit as successful as Land Rover had hoped. The long-term plan was for other Solihull products to follow it across the Atlantic, but the first-generation Discovery was never part of this. First priority was to relaunch the Land Rover brand on the back of the Range Rover's success,

and this was done in 1992. The company name was changed to Land Rover of North America, and a limited edition of 500 specially-equipped Defender 110 models was imported. Meanwhile, market research was giving Land Rover a clear idea of what US and Canadian customers might want in the Discovery. So these North American requirements were fed into the Romulus project, and the second-generation Discovery was prepared to suit American buyers as well as those in markets for the existing model.

The NAS Discovery
So the North American Specification (NAS) Discovery was developed as part of the Romulus project. It was influenced not only by customer

NAS prepares Discovery for North America

expectations – which affected the detail specification of the vehicle – but also by US legislation, which mostly affected exhaust emissions control and safety features.

As far as customer expectations were concerned, there would be no question of offering either the turbodiesel engine or the 2-litre Mpi petrol type. Buyers of medium-sized family 4x4s in North America had no interest in diesel power, and the MPi engine would be out of place in a market where engines of twice its cubic capacity were commonplace. So the 3.9-

Before the Discovery was announced in the USA, a group of North American-specification vehicles took part in the La Ruta Maya event, an eco-adventure in Belize which generated publicity for the new model.

This is one of the first (1994) North American models, with pewter-finish Castor alloy wheels. Note the side marker lights and the third stop lamp at the top of the tail door glass.

Canada received its first Discoverys in February 1995. They were essentially to US specification, but had detail differences. This is the first shipment to arrive, before being unloaded from the hold of the vessel *Auto Banner*.

With the 1996 range realignment came new decals, like these on an SD model, bottom of the range that year.

litre V8, already certified for use in the USA as part of the Range Rover programme, was to be the only choice.

The Range Rover had established Land Rover as a premium brand in North America, so it was important not to undermine this position, and no three-door Discovery was ever planned for the USA. Automatic transmission – already available – was expected to be the best-seller, although the five-speed manual would also be available initially in order to gauge demand. Luxury and convenience features like air

The challenge of US safety legislation

conditioning, central locking and electric windows had already been developed for the Discovery and of course would feature in the North American specification. What the Discovery did not yet have was leather upholstery, and so that was developed with the North American market in mind (although it also appeared in the range-topping ES derivative

in other countries).

Meeting emissions legislation was not a problem because the V8 engine was being kept in line with the latest requirements as part of the Range Rover programme. However, meeting North American safety legislation was more of a challenge. Features engineered into the second-generation Discovery specifically to suit Federal requirements were the crush cans at the front of the chassis, the side impact bars in the doors and, of course, the airbags. US models also had special lighting arrangements to meet local regulations. They had side marker lights in the front and rear bumper wraparounds, and they were the first Discoverys to have a third brake light mounted at the top of the tail door glass.

Other features, such as warning chimes for keys left in the ignition, were simpler to add. North American safety legislation also demanded such details as an inscription on the glass of each door mirror to remind the driver that objects which appeared in it were not full-size. A practical feature, never made available for other markets, was a receiver socket below the rear bumper for a detachable towbar.

La Ruta Maya

As the Discovery was a product line completely new to US buyers, it was introduced with a special publicity splash. Three months before its availability in US showrooms, it starred in an eco-adventure designed specifically to appeal to

72

The occasional seats were covered in leather, like the main seats, as this 1996 Canadian Discovery shows.

potential American buyers. This was known as La Ruta Maya – an Expedition of Discovery. The first half of that title translated as 'The Mayan Road' and linked the event to archeological research into the ancient Mayan civilization of Central America.

Recent research at an American University had discovered how to create authentic-looking replicas of ancient monuments from glassfibre, and a plan had been drawn up to take two such replicas back to the sites where the originals had been found at the heart of the former Mayan civilization in the jungle of Belize. Land Rover North America got together with the La Ruta Maya Conservation Foundation and agreed to sponsor the trip and to carry the replica artefacts to their destination by Discovery.

The expedition left Belize City on January 17 and returned a week later. At the departure ceremony, LRNA also presented the Conservation Foundation with an ex-Camel Trophy Discovery for use in its work. Eight of the new US-specification Discoverys were used

to take the replica artefacts down to Caracol, the ancient Mayan capital, and they also conveyed a team of archeologists, scientists and no fewer than 16 journalists, whose job was to publicize the trip. Nevertheless, Land Rover managed to keep details of the vehicles themselves out of the European press so that the launch in March lost none of its impact.

The first US Discoverys, 1994
LRNA announced the Discovery at the New York Auto Show early in 1994, and the new vehicles became available a few months later. Confusingly, the first Discoverys for the US market were 1994 models, even though their contemporaries sold elsewhere were called 1995 models, as were the new 'airbag' Range Rovers introduced at the same time!

Driver and passenger airbags were standard, and all US Discoverys were five-door models with the 182bhp 3.9-litre V8 engine and exhaust catalyst. The five-speed transmission was standard and the four-speed automatic an extra-

The 1997 Discovery SE had the deep-dish alloy wheels used on the XS in other markets. Note the wing decal here.

The 1997 models brought wood trim for the first time, as seen here on an SE7 model.

cost option. Castor alloy wheels with a pewter finish were standard wear, and all models came with ABS, cruise control and air conditioning. Trim was in beige fabric, with leather available at extra cost, while the inward-facing occasional rear seats and twin sunroofs were optional. Foglamps, the CD player and the retractable bumper step were also on the options list. At this stage, however, there were no Discoverys for Canada.

The 1995 Discovery
The Discovery went down a storm in the USA, proving to be another triumph for Land Rover. More than 4,000 had been sold by the time the mildly revised 1995 models reached the showrooms, and *Four-Wheeler* magazine awarded the new model its prestigious Four-Wheeler of the Year title. This was the second time a Land Rover product had been honoured in this way, for the title had gone to the Defender 90 a year earlier.

Feedback from early customers had also prompted some changes to the 1995-model Discoverys built for the USA and – from February 1995 – for Canada. Apart from two

Perhaps the most exciting among the 1997 models was the limited-edition Discovery XD. Finished in bright yellow and kitted out for off-road work, it certainly looked the part.

As the tailgate decal makes clear, the Discovery XD was built by Land Rover Special Vehicles. The wheels are Castor alloys, with a gunmetal finish.

new paint colours (Biarritz Blue and Epsom Green), the 1995 US models had side-impact beams in the rear doors as well as the fronts, Sparkle Silver (instead of pewter) wheel finish, an adjustable lumbar support pad in the front seats and a remote central locking transmitter which also activated the interior lights. American customers fell over themselves to buy Discoverys, and the question of numbers available for the US market was a major issue at the 1995 dealer conference held in Aspen, Colorado. Combined sales for the USA and Canada rose to an astonishing 10,552 units for the 1995 model-year.

The Discovery was also launched in Canada during February 1995. Canadian models had the same basic specification as US types, but also some unique features to suit local conditions. Thus they were equipped with a speedometer marked in kilometres per hour, a cylinder block heater, daytime running lights, and instructions in both French and English on their sun-visors to suit the country's dual-language population. Nevertheless it appears that there were no

---

Realignment boosts sales in USA and Canada

Canadian models with these instructions in Chinese, even though dealers in Toronto issued Chinese-language sales brochures to suit the area's large Chinese-speaking population!

Realignment for 1996

The 1996 model-year would prove to be the best for Discovery in the USA and Canada, with combined sales reaching 18,320 vehicles. This astonishing total reflected both improvements in the vehicles and a realignment of the range. For this year – and for 1997 – there were three basic models, ranging from the entry-level SD through the SE and up to the SE7. Each one was badged appropriately, although these badges were not the same as those used on the similarly-named models for Australia discussed in Chapter 6.

The SD retained the Castor alloy wheels and cloth upholstery available on 1996 models, although it did take on several other new features which were common across the 1997 range. These were an automatic dimming rear-view mirror (seen before on Range Rovers),

illuminated vanity mirrors for both driver and passenger, and additional speakers on the windscreen pillars (again a feature seen before on Range Rovers). There were three new colours across the range, of which Altai Silver came with Granite trim in cloth or leather instead of the standard Bahama Beige.

The SE and SE7 both came with leather upholstery, twin sunroofs and eight-way power-adjustable front seats as standard. Both also had five-spoke Freestyle Choice alloy wheels. The SE7, as its name suggested, was a seven-seater model with the inward-facing occasional rear seats as standard. These were accompanied by a separate rear air conditioning unit, mounted on the rear of the centre console. All this extra equipment made a difference to the weight, too, and the kerb weight of a 1996 North American Discovery was 4,465lb (2,025kg) as against 4,379lb (1,986kg) for the previous year's models.

Most interesting of this season's changes, however, was that the North American Discovery switched from the 3.9-litre V8 engine to the newer '4.0-litre' type which had been introduced in the second-generation Range Rover during 1994. This version of the engine, known to Land Rover as the RV8, would never be seen in Discoverys for other markets, and was introduced mainly as a cost-saving measure, so that Land Rover no longer had to submit two versions of the same engine for certification with the Federal authorities every year.

The 4.0-litre V8 in fact had the same 3,947cc swept volume as the older engine (even though Land Rover tended to quote the figure as 3,950cc), but it had been completely redesigned and almost every component had been either modified or changed. Many of these changes had been brought about as part of the development of the Range Rover's 4.6-litre engine, and they included a new cylinder block with additional stiffening ribs and modifications to accommodate larger-diameter main bearings with cross-bolted bearing caps. All components ahead of the front face of the cylinder block had also been redesigned to reduce engine length by 75mm (2.95in), and this redesign had led to greater refinement, improved engine durability and reduced service requirements. They were driven by a single poly-vee belt, which replaced the multiple belts of the earlier engine.

Instead of the Lucas-Bosch injection system of the 3.9-litre engine, the 4.0-litre type had a new engine management system known as GEMS (Generic Engine Management System) which had been developed jointly by Land Rover and Segam Lucas. This had sophisticated features like knock sensing and automatic timing adjustment to compensate, and instead of a conventional distributor and HT leads, it

used four double-ended ignition coils for greater reliability. As far as the North American market was concerned, it also brought small but welcome improvements in the fuel economy figures calculated by the Environmental Protection Agency.

Improvements for 1997

Thus distinguished from Discoverys for all other countries, the North American vehicles entered the 1997 season, when there were further improvements all round in the three-model range. Three more new colours were introduced, along with a darker window tint as standard, and the radio now had a diversity antenna implanted in the side glass so there was no need for a mast aerial. All models had California Walnut wood trim on the dashboard, and all of them had the latest LT230 Q version of Land Rover's venerable gear-driven transfer box. The Q was supposed to stand for Quiet, and the new box certainly was quieter than the old, thanks to deeper teeth on the high-range gearwheels. In addition, a simplifed airbag operating system was introduced.

The SD model lost its Castor wheels and took on the Freestyle Choice type of the more expensive 1996 models, while the SE and SE7 both moved on to have deep-dish alloy wheels. These two models could also be fitted with HomeLink – a remote control for garage doors, gates and house lighting which was mounted above the rear-view mirror.

The 1997 season also brought three limited editions. The most spectacular of these was undoubtedly the Discovery XD, of which 250 were built for the USA and a further 25 for Canada. This was a Special Vehicles confection, and carried the badges to prove it. Finished in AA Yellow, a colour not otherwise available on Discoverys for any market, the XD was essentially an SE-specification automatic equipped with gunmetal-coloured Castor wheels, a skid plate, lamp guards, a roof rack and some fairly extrovert identification. Ten XDs were used on that year's TReK, which publicity described as 'a Camel Trophy-like competition for retailer teams', and a further 28 on the Eco-Challenge, which was an eight-day endurance event held in British Columbia. The TReK and Eco-Challenge vehicles carried extra identification.

The second limited edition was launched in March 1997, when 500 North American Discoverys were equipped with the Kit Trail Package. First introduced in California, this had spread to the other states and also became available in Canada. The package consisted of a front A-bar, roof ladder, lamp guards, and bodyside and wheelarch protective mouldings, all finished in Satin Black, together with driving lights and a new spare wheel cover with rigid rim and soft centre.

The third limited edition arrived late in the

1998 brought the Discovery LSE, with chromed bumpers among its distinguishing features.

season when Land Rover North America and Land Rover Canada previewed the 1998 models with a new top-of-the-range Discovery called the LSE. Based on the SE, this came in one of two new colours (White Gold or British Racing Green), and in either case it had an interior trimmed in Lightstone leather, another colour new to the North American market.

Fewer models but more equipment cross the Atlantic

The run-out models

However, the 1997 season had not been as successful as the previous one for Discovery across the Atlantic. So for 1998, the range in the USA was trimmed down to two models, which were badged as the LE and LSE. At $34,500, the LE was priced mid-way between the old SD and SE, while the LSE at $38,000 was actually $500

cheaper than the 1997 SE7. It was a clever strategy: at first glance, it looked as if the Discovery had become even more exclusive and upmarket, whereas in reality the range had simply lost its bottom end and showroom prices had gone down.

Automatic transmission and leather upholstery were standard on both LE and LSE, although in Canada there was still an entry-level Discovery SD with the five-speed manual gearbox and cloth trim. Once again there were new colours and features, of which the most welcome to many buyers must have been the extension of the warranty period from three to four years. Both models now had map lights on the auto-dimming interior mirror, and the door trims were more elaborate. Either could be ordered with the seven-seat option at extra cost, but only the LSE came with a 240-watt Harman Kardon ICE with eight speakers and a six-disc CD changer. The LE had the deep-dish alloy wheels of the 1997 SE and SE7, but the LSE had a new satin-finish, five-spoke style known as Boost, with recessed sculpted spokes. This had the so-called 'jewelled' centre caps, carrying a coloured Land Rover logo.

The LSE remained the only North American Discovery to have Lightstone leather upholstery, and for 1998 it also had additional wood trim as

The LSE had special badges and new Boost alloy wheels.

There were just 50 '50th Anniversary Edition' models in 1998, and they carried this decal on the tailgate and below the rear side windows. There was also a numbered brass plaque on the dashboard.

well as leather for the handbrake and gear-lever gaiters. There were bright stainless steel kick-plates and door handles, and stainless steel was also used for the bumpers – as it had been on top-model North American Range Rovers at the

Clearing the way for the new Discovery

beginning of the decade. The radiator grille, spoiler, bumper end caps and mirror bodies were all painted in the body colour, and the bump-strip along the side had a bright insert, again echoing Range Rover practice of many years earlier.

Land Rover North America and Land Rover Canada both capitalized on the 50th Anniversary of the Land Rover marque during 1998 by selling examples of a special limited-edition model. Introduced towards the end of the season, this was finished in metallic Woodcote Green – one of the colours new for 1998 – and was essentially an LE model with special decals, Lightstone leather upholstery and a numbered brass plate. Not surprisingly, the edition was limited to 50 examples.

The 1998 models, of course, were the last of their type to reach North America, and their task was to prepare the way for the much-improved new Discovery, which would be launched as a 1999 model. Land Rover North America had predicted a further drop in sales for 1998, because American customers were impatient for something new. A great deal of the effort which had gone into the 1999 Discovery had been influenced by feedback from US and Canadian customers, and Land Rover could only hope that it would bring about a recovery in sales volumes.

CHAPTER 8

THE TEMPEST PROJECT

Redeveloping a class leader

No matter how good a product may be, its makers cannot afford to stand still. Sooner or later a rival manufacturer will develop a product which is equally good, cheaper, or even better, and so it was with the Discovery. By the mid-1990s, Land Rover's best-seller was coming under increasing pressure from newer vehicles aimed at the same group of potential buyers. The Jeep Grand Cherokee, the new Nissan Patrol, the Toyota 90-series Land Cruiser (known in some countries as the Colorado) and the Mercedes-Benz M-class had all started to eat into sales of the Discovery, which began to drop in 1996 and dropped further in 1997.

However, Land Rover had never had any intention of letting the Discovery wither on the vine. As soon as the Romulus project had been signed off for production, work began on a third-generation Discovery under project leader Nick Fell. It was code-named Tempest, and from the beginning it was clear that this vehicle would have to take the Discovery range further upmarket in order to leave ample room for the forthcoming Freelander as the new entry-level model in the Land Rover range. As a result, it was decided that the new Discovery would be available only as a five-door model, and as this would mean the demise of the Discovery Commercial, which was based on the three-door body, plans were made for a commercial version of the Freelander to replace it.

From market research, Land Rover knew that customers were broadly happy with the Discovery as it was. They liked its distinctive shape and expressed the hope that this would be retained in any future updates. However, they rated its handling as poor, they were unhappy with its sometimes questionable build quality, and although they admired the fuel economy of the turbodiesel engine, they also thought it was

noisier than many rivals. Despite the image which the Discovery had acquired in some areas as a shopping-trolley for wealthy men's wives, market research showed that an astonishing 23 per cent of potential customers expected to use their vehicles off-road at least once a week.

The design team also had to take into consideration the special demands of the North American market. At one end of the spectrum were small niggles, such as the difficulty of seeing overhead traffic signals because of the position of the windscreen brow, and at the other end were forthcoming legislative issues

---

New owner BMW gives go-ahead for five-cylinder diesel

---

about safety belts, which would outlaw the lap belts fitted to the centre of the rear bench and to the occasional seats in the load area.

These factors all had an influence on the shape of Project Tempest. In the meantime, work was going ahead on engine development for the whole of the Land Rover range. The venerable V8 petrol engine, available in Defender, Discovery and Range Rover, was moving to the next stage of its existence with the design of a new twin-plenum inlet manifold code-named Thor. As for diesels, the Gemini range had reached the limit of its development, and a new modular family of four, five and six-

The ACE suspension planned for the Tempest vehicle was tested on old-model Discoverys. This one was pictured in the late summer of 1995. Note the Range Rover wheels – a giveaway to observers because they would not fit the pre-1998 Discovery axles! A close look reveals that an extra panel has been inserted just behind the rear window to increase the length to that planned for Tempest.

First public airing for the new Discovery was on April 30, 1998, when Land Rover North America showed an example briefly at their 50th Anniversary celebrations in Lanham. *(Picture by courtesy of Ken Watkin.)*

The wider track made the new Discovery appear lower and more sporting.

The extra length was hard to spot at a quick glance, even though it tended to make the model look both lower and sleeker, an impression aided by the raised belt-line indentation.

The ACE hydraulics which operated on the front anti-roll bar can be seen clearly in this view of a demonstration chassis.

cylinder engines was being planned for use in Rover cars and Land Rovers. The BMW takeover in 1994 caused the cancellation of the four-cylinder and six-cylinder variants, because the German company was already developing such engines itself. However, the Land Rover engineers were encouraged to pursue the five-cylinder version of the design for their own vehicles, and work on this went ahead under the project name Storm.

Chassis-frame and suspension

The requirement to improve the Discovery's on-road dynamics went hand in hand with the necessity of retaining its excellent off-road ability. To meet both criteria, the Land Rover engineers put together a complex package of inter-related improvements.

Fundamental to this was a completely new chassis which would increase the rigidity of the whole vehicle. Still of box-section ladder-frame design, it nevertheless had six cross-members instead of the five of the original Range Rover-derived type. The number of body mounting points was increased to 14, again to improve overall rigidity. New steering geometry was devised, drawing inspiration from the system used on the new Range Rover introduced in 1994. For the front axle of Tempest, the engineers used Range Rover-style open yoke universal joints, thus altering the kingpin inclination to the benefit of overall steering feel and reducing steering kickback from rough ground or braking forces.

Wider front and rear axles were chosen to improve the general stability and roadholding, and the suspension linkages were completely redesigned. The original A-frame location of the rear axle was abandoned in favour of a Watts linkage, which reduced cornering roll by raising the roll-centre height. Meanwhile, a modified Panhard rod was used on the front axle, and new suspension bush arrangements front and rear allowed better axle control. All these changes, used with the existing all-round coil-spring suspension, resulted in much tighter handling for the new Discovery.

However, for the more expensive models (and,

as usual, as an option on the others), Land Rover went one better. They developed an active ride control system to minimize the Discovery's characteristic cornering roll. This was christened ACE, or Active Cornering Enhancement, by the marketing men. It operated through a pair of lateral g-force sensors, which acted on a hydraulic pump connected to the ends of the front and rear anti-roll bars. As soon as the sensors detected the beginning of body roll in a bend, fluid was pumped through the pipework to 'stiffen' the anti-roll bar on the outside of the bend and thus to allow the vehicle to corner almost flat. Interlinking ensured the system was deactivated at low speeds so that the long wheel travel which had been a traditional Discovery strength off-road was not compromised. The handling of the new Discovery when equipped with ACE was quite extraordinary for a vehicle of its type, and was in a completely different league from that of its predecessors.

The new chassis had to have a longer rear overhang than the old to allow a longer body, which gave room for the forward-facing occasional seats. This longer rear overhang, of course, reduced the departure angle, allowing the rear to ground earlier as the vehicle went from level ground on to a steep incline. So for all variants except the entry-level models,

Solihull's engineers devised an ingenious air spring system which would lift the rear of the body higher above the axle, so restoring the departure angle.

The air springs, which replaced the standard coil springs on the rear axle, were also designed to act as self-levellers and to maintain the ride height at the rear when the vehicle was fully laden. The system was known by the acronym of

---

SLS and a party trick for Discovery trailer pullers

SLS (Self Levelling Suspension), and it brought the additional benefit of allowing the rear of the vehicle to be lowered when it was being hitched to a trailer. As an option, a remote-control handset was designed so that this party trick could be performed while the driver was outside, actually hitching the trailer to the towbar.

The valve block for the ACE system was on the right-hand chassis rail. The two lateral acceleration sensors were on the left-hand chassis rail and between the roof and headlining.

Model-designations were retained from the old Discovery. This is a top-of-the range ES, with the wheelarch cladding fitted to both this and XS models.

Traction and braking aids

The Land Rover armoury already included ABS – seen on ES models of the second-generation Discovery – which was a much more complex anti-lock braking system than normal car types, using four separate channels and being designed for use off-road as well as on the road. It also included Electronic Traction Control (ETC), which was used on the rear axle of the Range Rover and operated through the ABS system. If one rear wheel lost traction, the ABS wheel sensor told an electronic brain which braked that wheel and thus transferred all the drive to the opposite wheel through the action of the differential.

The Land Rover engineers took this technology a stage further for the new Discovery. ABS became standard equipment, and ETC was made to operate on all four wheels, with the result that the vehicle could find traction if only one of its wheels had grip. This very effectively duplicated the action of a locking centre differential, so this feature was deleted from the transfer gearbox – saving both weight and cost.

The basic ABS system was also harnessed to two other systems, the first being Electronic Brake Distribution (EBD), which prevented the rear brakes locking up under weight transfer forward during heavy braking and also ensured that uneven weight distribution in the vehicle

did not affect the braking performance. The second was Hill Descent Control (HDC), which had first been seen on the Freelander. HDC was designed for off-road use, and used the ABS to slow the speed of the vehicle's descent on a steep slope off-road in order to prevent either a runaway or a loss of stability, resulting in a sudden rear-end breakaway. However, in the Freelander, HDC had been used instead of a low range of gears; in the new Discovery, it was used in addition to the traditional transfer gearbox giving High and Low ranges.

Powertrains

The Storm five-cylinder turbodiesel engine developed for the new Discovery represented a massive advance on the Gemini four-cylinders in terms of responsiveness and refinement. With it came the new designation of Td5, applied to both engine and vehicle in place of the earlier Tdi designation. In some aspects of its design, it was closely related to the 2-litre L-series diesel engine used in Rover cars and the Freelander, and during development the engineers had taken care to use common components – such as con-rods – wherever possible.

Like the earlier Tdi power units, the Storm engine had a swept volume of 2,495cc, which was important in order to remain under the tax-break size of 2.5 litres in Italy, the major Land

Visible in this picture of the 4.0-litre V8 engine are the curved pipes of the new Thor inlet manifold.

Rover diesel market. Maximum power was 136bhp, some 22.5 per cent up on the Tdi units, which of course gave the new Discovery a higher maximum speed. Equally important, however, were the increased torque and flatter torque curve. Whereas the Tdi had developed 195lb.ft at 1,800rpm, the Td5 boasted 221lb.ft (232lb.ft with automatic transmission), still developed at the low engine speed of 1,950rpm. All of 90 per cent of that torque was available as low as 1,450rpm, and the torque spread was extended so that at least 80 per cent of the maximum was available between 1,300 and 3,900rpm. With a governed speed of 4,850rpm – high for a diesel – the Td5 drove like a gutsy petrol engine.

Central to the creation of the Storm engine was the adoption of Lucas Electronic Unit Injectors in place of the direct-injection system of the Gemini units. Already proven in large truck diesels, the EUI system used an individual camshaft-driven plunger pump for each cylinder's injector, with ultra-precise electronic control of the injection period and timing. The system was able to operate at very high pressures – typically around two and a half times as great as those used in the Tdi's direct injection – which contributed to good control of exhaust emissions. As a result, the Storm engine met all existing and anticipated diesel emissions regulations worldwide without the need for an exhaust catalyst.

The whole fuelling of the engine was controlled by a powerful new electronic Engine Control Module (ECM), developed under the code-name of Thunder and linked into other electronic control units on the vehicle. These included the automatic transmission and air conditioning when fitted, the ABS, SLS, Body Control Unit and a safety inertia switch which would cut off the fuel supply in a collision.

The V8 petrol engine was also developed further, to improve refinement, give a wider torque spread, and meet new legislation in some

The five-cylinder Td5 engine was a quantum leap ahead of the superseded 300Tdi in terms of refinement.

of the vehicle's markets. However, while the Thor engine undoubtedly brought the by-now elderly design up to modern standards, by comparison with the changes between the Tdi and Td5 engines it was a disappointment. As far as American Discoverys were concerned, it represented one step ahead of the 4.0-litre V8 which they had used since mid-1995. For the rest of the world, however, it was two steps ahead of the 3.9-litre V8 in the outgoing models, because the 4.0-litre engine had been an intermediate development.

New inlet manifolding was the main cause of a torque increase of nearly 9 per cent, at 500rpm lower in the speed range than on the superseded 3.9-litre engine. This improved acceleration from rest as well as response at motorway cruising speeds, while an improved spread of torque resulted in more relaxed performance. Maximum power was also slightly increased, from 180bhp (134Kw) to 182bhp (136Kw) at the same 4,750rpm.

Other improvements for the V8 included the adoption of Bosch Motronic 5.2.1 engine management, similar to that used on the BMW 7 and 8 series models. This system enabled the engine to meet the latest American requirements for on-board diagnostics. The ignition system, with four coils and no distributor, now used long-life double-platinum spark plugs with a maintenance-free life of 72,000 miles (116,000km). As on the earlier RV8 4.0-litre engine, cross-bolted main bearing caps were used, and in addition there was a new structural cast alloy sump to improve refinement. Yet again, the front end auxiliary drive arrangements were altered, this time with four different colour-coded poly-vee belts to suit different combinations of ancillaries.

Customer demand ensured that both manual and automatic gearboxes would again be available with both engines. There would also be the familiar dual-range transfer gearbox, although without the locking centre differential

The dashboard was subtly different from the superseded type. This is the top-specification ES, with automatic air conditioning and 320-watt Harman/Kardon ICE system.

of earlier models because of the new four-wheel ETC technology. The manual gearbox was the familiar five-speed R380, on which quality control had been tightened to eliminate the problems experienced in the mid-1990s. The automatic chosen was also familiar to a degree, as it was once again a four-speed ZF type. However, for the new Discovery it had electro-hydraulic control and a switchable Sport mode like that on the Range Rover, which allowed the engine to hang on to lower gears for longer to improve acceleration and made the kickdown more responsive. The new transmission was known by the rather cumbersome name of 4HP22EH.

An additional refinement for the powertrain was an electronic throttle, which incorporated Anti-Shunt Control (ASC). This smoothed out the action of the throttle so that sudden inputs would not produce the drivetrain shunt which had been a feature of every earlier Discovery and every Range Rover before that. It was not completely foolproof, but it did remove one other difference between the behaviour of the Discovery and that of the conventional estates with which it had to compete.

Body exterior
The body designers under Alan Mobberley had an extremely difficult task to perform as their brief was to retain the existing appearance of the

Discovery and yet to modify it to suit the wider axles and longer rear overhang specified for Tempest. They also had to incorporate minor improvements like Range Rover-style door handles and a lower mounting position for the spare wheel. In the event, they made so many changes that every exterior panel bar one – the tailgate skin – was different. There were new structural elements under the skin, too, and the completed Tempest shell incorporated some 200 new pressings and 100 modified or carry-over items.

This retooling of the bodyshell allowed much higher standards of manufacture, and the new tools were designed to eliminate the poor fits and large panel gaps of earlier Discoverys. Ease of manufacture had also been an important factor in the design and had resulted in a reduced panel count and simplification. Thus, for example, the new extended rear floor structure was a single pressing instead of seven in the earlier vehicle. An additional benefit of all this was a stiffer bodyshell.

There were changes in the body materials, too. Zinc-coated steel was used extensively in the lower part of the shell, and the door skins were made of steel rather than the traditional aluminium alloy in order to achieve easier manufacture and tighter tolerances. This time around, much higher manufacturing volumes were allowed for to avoid the quality control

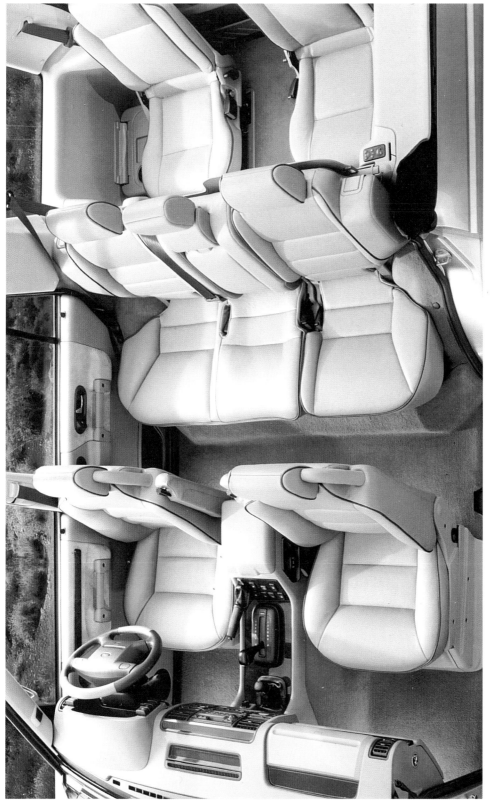

The leather seats on top models had contrasting piping, and there was a head restraint for the central passenger in the second row. The third row occasional seats had their own headphones and volume controls, the latter just visible behind the backrest of the second-row seats.

problems which had arisen when production of the earlier models increased beyond the planned estimates.

The new Discovery was not easy to distinguish from the old at a glance, but there were certain key differences. The front was completely revised, with a new bumper-and-spoiler assembly, a body-coloured three-quarter frame for the grille, and round headlamp reflectors within the rectangular apertures. From the side, the most obvious differences were the new door handles, the raised styling crease along the flanks, and the changed D and E-pillars, which betrayed the longer rear overhang. The rear side windows and Alpine lights were also direct-glazed to the bodyshell and lacked the protruding rubber seals of earlier models. From behind, the most obvious difference was that the new tail-lamp clusters were mounted higher up the body sides. The cutouts for the bumper-mounted lamps were also more rounded, and the spare wheel sat closer to the bumper. Colours were also new, particularly striking among them being a burnt orange micatallic

---

Tempest becomes a lower and sportier Discovery

---

colour called Kinversand and a silver sheen called Blenheim.

Overall, the Tempest redesign made the Discovery appear lower and more sporting – especially when the optional 18-inch alloy wheels and low-profile tyres were specified. Wheels, of course, are an important part of a vehicle's appearance, and all styles were new and – because of the new axles – not interchangeable with those on earlier Discovery models. Standard wheels were 16-inch five-spoke alloys; 18-inch five-spokes were optional on lesser models and standard on higher-specification types, and it was possible to order the stylish 18-inch Mondial star-pattern alloys introduced earlier on the Range Rover.

Body interior

Like the exterior, the interior of the Discovery was substantially redesigned for Tempest, but the visible changes were not immediately obvious. They started with the facia, where there was a new instrument pack with an electronic speedometer and a Message Centre similar to the one pioneered in the Range Rover from 1994. The new steering wheel was more substantial in appearance, with the 'jewelled' Land Rover badge in its centre.

Dial controls for the heater were retained, allowing driver and passenger to select different temperatures, but standard on ES models and optional elsewhere was a version of the automatic air conditioning system used on the Range Rover. This allowed the selected temperature – hot or cold – to be maintained automatically. Rear air conditioning was available again, but this time it operated through overhead vents instead of from a separate box on the rear of the centre console.

While the Bahama Beige interior colour was carried over from the old vehicle, a new Dark Smokestone was introduced as the alternative. Leather remained available on the top-model ES or as an option, but it now came with contrasting piping and Alcantara accent panels on the door casings. Lightstone leather was a special option. On the entry-level and S models, new Cumbria and Carlisle cloth fabrics were introduced, while the XS retained its part-leather trim but with the latest fabrics.

The seats were also redesigned, those at the front having wider, deeper and more shapely cushions and squabs on new frames, together with car-type height-adjustable head restraints. There was also an adjustable lumbar pad, similar to that pioneered on the Freelander. Side grips retained the 'golf-ball' textures associated with the Discovery since its introduction, but they were much less noticeable than before. At the rear, the seat retained its 60/40 split folding feature, but was now latched to the floor rather than to the body sides. The squabs were taller and more supportive, and the side cushion profile was modified to ease entry to the seat.

The centre rear seat was provided with a three-point inertia-reel belt instead of the lap belt on earlier Discoverys, and it had an ingenious headrest arrangement. Naturally, when the seat was occupied the central armrest was folded up, and the action of stowing it raised its headrest into position. When the seat was not occupied, the central armrest could be folded down and the headrest would slide down with it, thus reducing obstruction in the rear-view mirror.

Most striking of the interior changes, however, was to the occasional rear seats, which were standard equipment on all except the entry-level models. These now faced forwards instead of inwards, yet still hinged out from the sides of the load bay, where they were stored out of the way when not in use. They had a clever locking mechanism which latched them in position on the floor, and they were provided

Visible here are the locking catches in the rear floor for the foldaway third-row seats, and the ingenious head restraint, which folded up into the roof when not in use.

with drop-down head restraints which stowed under the roof above the rear door. Both seats had proper three-point inertia-reel seat belts in place of the earlier lap belts. The light colour of the headlining was also extended down to waist level to give an airier ambience in the rear. However, there was no denying that legroom in these occasional seats was insufficient for adults on a long journey, despite the increased length in the rear part of the vehicle.

Of course, the occasional rear seats were traditionally the preserve of children travelling in a Discovery, and on some models the ICE system was wired to a control unit ahead of each seat, which was provided with a pair of headphones. The idea was that children in the back could listen to their choice of entertainment (a CD, for example) while the main speakers were playing the driver's choice (the radio or a tape).

Security was also improved. The volumetric sensing was enhanced, and there was a superlock setting which disabled all the interior door handles and the sill buttons. At the same time, the engine immobilizer was made easier to use by means of a transponder built into the ignition key. The vehicle interrogated the transponder, and if satisfied that this was the correct key, it automatically disabled the immobilizer as the key was turned.

The sophisticated mechanism of the new Discovery exposed. This artist's drawing depicts a vehicle powered by the latest 2.5-litre direct-injection five-cylinder diesel engine coupled to the ZF electronically controlled automatic gearbox.

Model line-up

For most markets, the new Discovery was offered in four different specification levels: base, S, XS and ES. The base models did not have the new suspension system or the seven-seat configuration, and they had cloth upholstery and 16-inch wheels. The S models, which were expected to be the most popular, had both the new suspension and the seven seats. The XS, as before, was the sporty model and came with the new suspension and seven seats. The ES, as the top model, had seven leather-trimmed seats, automatic air conditioning, 18-inch wheels and the new suspension.

The new Discovery range was previewed in the USA at a special Land Rover 50th Anniversary celebration held on April 30, 1998 at Land Rover North America's Lanham headquarters. In June, a pair of Blenheim Silver models – one V8i and one Td5 – set off on a round-the-world publicity trip which covered 19,152 miles and 27 countries in 58 days. In early August, a technical briefing day on the new vehicle was held for invited members of the world's media at the Rover Group's Gaydon research and development centre. A ride-and-drive event for the press followed during September near Nairn, in the Scottish Highlands, and the vehicle was finally revealed to the public at the Paris motor show on September 29. Sales would begin on November 21 in the UK, and in the New Year elsewhere.

The Land Rover designers and engineers had done all they could. The world's media had given their unanimous approval to the biggest series of changes in the history of the Discovery. Now it was up to the buyers to prove that the new model was right on target, just as its predecessors had been.

CHAPTER 9

SPECIAL DERIVATIVES

Adapted Discoverys since 1989

Ever since the marque's earliest days, Land Rover's products have been conceived as basic 'platforms' which can be customized to suit the buyer's requirements. The first specially-adapted vehicle was the Mobile Welder, introduced in 1948 as a variant of the line-built 80-inch model, and over the years the number of specialist adaptations of the Land Rover grew and grew. In the mid-1950s, the Rover Company tried to assert control over aftermarket conversions through the Land Rover Approval scheme and by the creation of the Special Projects Department, the distant ancestor of today's Land Rover Special Vehicles. And as soon as the Range Rover had been signed off for production, the Special Projects engineers started to find ways of adapting the basic vehicle to different purposes. So it was no surprise when the same process was applied to the Discovery soon after its launch in 1989.

The first adaptations of the Range Rover had turned it into an emergency service vehicle for Police, fire and ambulance work, and Land Rover followed much the same strategy for the Discovery. In fact, the plan to develop special versions of the Discovery was closely bound up with Land Rover's overall product development plan. The Range Rover was to be moved further upmarket to become a luxury car alternative (in preparation for the 1994 arrival of the second-generation model), and Land Rover believed its image would be harmed if low-specification variants continued to be available for emergency service use. So the Discovery was to replace it as a platform for the specialist converters.

Police and ambulance variants of the Discovery were swiftly developed to replace their Range Rover forebears, although a Tdi-powered Police-specification Range Rover continued to be available alongside the Police-specification

Discovery until 1994. Land Rover stopped supplying Range Rover chassis to be converted into six-wheel fire tenders after about 1990, but in this case the Defender 130 was moved into the gap in order to save the cost of developing an additional Discovery variant.

The Police Discovery

The Discovery was ideally suited to Police work with a minimum of modification. Police Forces all over Britain and in several other countries were already familiar with its mechanical elements because these had already been seen in the Range Rovers they had bought. The

Range Rovers give way to Police Discoverys

Discovery brought the additional advantage of a more accessible loadspace in the rear, so all that was needed was some racking for equipment stowage, some additional wiring for lights, sirens and two-way radios, and a selection of the heavy-duty components already available on Police-specification Range Rovers.

The first Police-specification Discovery entered service with the Dyfed Powys Police in November 1990 and was a three-door model. It was followed by a rash of others, as Police Forces all over Britain rushed to add Discoverys to their motorway patrol fleets. The standard Police-specification Discovery was usually based

This one was not available to the public! Built in 1990 by SVO for publicity purposes at Cowes Week, which Land Rover sponsored that year, it floated by courtesy of technology developed on military prototypes in the early 1960s.

on the three-door model, not least because the base vehicle cost less than a five-door, and the vast majority built before the beginning of 1994 had the 200Tdi intercooled turbodiesel engine.

Nevertheless, five-door Police-specification Discoverys were delivered to the Thames Valley Police, among others, and it appears that some Police Forces created their own patrol vehicles from standard five-door models. These seem to have used the wiring harness developed for Police-specification Discoverys by SVO (Special Vehicle Operations, which took over from the Special Projects Department and lasted until the formation of Land Rover Special Vehicles in 1992).

Ambulance Discoverys

The Range Rover ambulance had always been based on a stretched wheelbase of 110 inches, and Land Rover's SVO division decided to replace this with a stretched-wheelbase Discovery. However, whereas the Range Rover chassis had always been converted by Spencer Abbott in Birmingham, the Discovery chassis would be converted by SVO in line with Land Rover's 1990s policy of keeping more conversion work in-house.

Land Rover's research had made clear that the market for a long-wheelbase all-terrain ambulance had altered since the Range Rover ambulances had been designed in the early 1970s. By the early 1990s, ambulance services were making increasing use of fast-response paramedic vehicles, so the new Discovery ambulance was drawn up with that requirement in mind. As SVO Director Alan Edis explained

Peter Hobson's camera caught this Discovery demonstrator at a British military exhibition in the early 1990s, but the vehicle was never popular with military users.

Land Rover built their own Police demonstrators very early on, but the first Discovery to enter Police service was this one, a three-door bought by the Dyfed Powys Police in Wales during 1990. In later years, the four-door Police Discovery would become a common sight on British motorways, where it took over from the Range Rover.

The Paramedic Discovery was built on a stretched wheelbase of 116 inches. This demonstrator, based on an early two-door model, shows off the interior accommodation.

when the new Paramedic Discovery was announced at the Ambex 91 exhibition on August 16, 1991:

'Before any attempt was made to create a paramedic version of the Discovery, we spent a lot of time examining the needs of individual ambulance services, and carefully balanced many of the recommendations made by the Association of Chief Ambulance Officers against our research.'

The result was a vehicle even bigger than the Range Rover ambulances, with a wheelbase 116 inches long. It was available with either the 200Tdi or injected 3.5-litre V8 engine, and could be adapted fairly comprehensively to suit the requirements of individual customers. About a year later, SVO also made available a Discovery ambulance conversion on the standard 100-inch wheelbase, which was rather cheaper, but of course much less roomy than the 116-inch type. This looked like the standard production vehicle, except that it had opaque glass in the rear.

The military Discovery

A number of civilian Discoverys which had been sold in Saudi Arabia were pressed into service by the Coalition Forces during the Gulf War of 1990-91. They greatly impressed those military commanders who had access to them, and Land Rover capitalized on this by showing 'military commander's vehicles' at military equipment shows after the war was over. Details of military contracts are always kept secret, and it is not clear whether the Discovery did find any military buyers in the period up to 1994.

During 1993, a press photographer also caught on film an interesting Land Rover prototype which had the front panels of a

Discovery prototype has press and photographers guessing

Discovery and the back body of a Defender HCPU. This was camouflaged with desert-colour military paint and carried the Coalition Forces' distinctive inverted 'V' on the sides of its tilt cover. There was speculation at the time that a Discovery pick-up was on the way, but the truth was rather more prosaic. Land Rover's product planners had suggested that it might be possible to update the Defender and simultaneously save manufacturing costs by giving Defenders the front panels of the Discovery, so a prototype was built to test the idea. However, the plan did not progress beyond the feasibility prototype, which

ortunately, this shot was
taged for the camera, but it
hows a different version of the
iscovery ambulance, this time
ased on a four-door body.

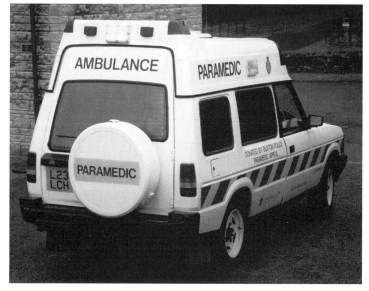

he Derbyshire Ambulance
ervice bought this Paramedic
iscovery in 1994, ordering a
pecial high-roof design.
Picture by courtesy of Alastair
reen.)

as revealed in 'scoop' pictures printed in a
umber of motoring magazines.

he Swiss utilities
evertheless, a Discovery utility model did

become available in Switzerland as early as
1991. During the previous decade, the Swiss
market had been a strong one for alloy-bodied
flat-bed and tipper coversions of the Land Rover
One Ten, but new noise and emissions

regulations effective from 1989 meant that the vehicle could no longer be sold in Switzerland. Keen not to lose their grip on a lucrative market, Land Rover Switzerland got agreement to offer these bodies on Discovery chassis instead.

The coversion work was carried out by the well-kown firm of Emil Frey, at Safenwil. The whole of the Dicovery front end and fron cabin was retained, with the rear of the cabin being formed by a ribbed metal sheet containing a single-pane window. Two chassis lengths were available, both of them with a wheelbase stretched by 500mm to 3,040mm (119.68in). The shorter one had a 1-metre (39.37in) overhang behind the rear axle, and the longer an 1,140mm (44.88in) overhang. The shorter chassis was normally used for the hydraulic tipper conversion, which had drop-sides as well as a hinged tailgate on a tipping body 1,970mm (77.56in) long.

The wheelchair carrier

Shortly after SVO was renamed as Land Rover

Discovery Commercial points way to tax exemption

Special Vehicles in 1992, the division announced yet another special Discovery, this time a version modified to carry a wheelchair. Most vehicles modified for this purpose were based on car-derived vans, such as Rover's Metro and the Ford Escort; the Discovery conversion was inevitably much more expensive than these, but was expected to have extra appeal because of its commanding height.

The wheelchair carrier Discovery featured a raised roof section in order to provide adequate headroom for a wheelchair-bound passenger in the back. Appropriate fixing points in the rear load floor ensured that the wheelchair would be safely located, and a hydraulic tail-lift of the kind used on ambulances for the disabled was fitted at the rear.

The Discovery Commercial

Before Land Rover Special Vehicles managed to get a van version of the Discovery onto the market in April 1993, such vehicles had already been introduced to the Irish market through the initiative of Stuarts Garages in Dublin. The advantage of the van conversion in Eire was tha it avoided the Import Motor Tax, which the added more than 40 per cent to the price of new vehicle, and thus brought the cost of three-door Discovery down to acceptable level for commercial users.

The Stuarts conversion was being advertise by Christmas 1990 and quickly proved popula with long waiting lists of up to three months fo new vehicles. It was a fairly straightforwar conversion of the three-door Discovery involving the removal of the rear seat and th blanking-out of all side windows behind th doors. Irish regulations of the time als demanded that the Alpine lights were blanke out. Around 350 examples were sold before ne regulations, introduced on January 1, 199: priced the vehicle out of the market by a chang in tax regulations which saw the introduction c Vehicle Registration Tax in place of Impor Motor Tax.

Meanwhile, LRSV had been working on thei own Discovery van, which was introduced i April 1993 under the name Discover Commercial. Land Rover's own van had bee designed to be exempt from tax in as man countries of the world as possible. Essentiall the LRSV vehicle was a base-specification thre door Discovery Tdi which had been stripped c its rear seats and fitted with a bulkhead behin the front seats, while the side windows behin the doors were blanked off. The first example were available in just four colours: Savari White, Eskdale Green, Corrallin Red an Windjammer Blue.

Even so, examples sold in Ireland had t incorporate certain modifications to qualify a commercial vehicles and thus for exemptio from Vehicle Registration Tax. Irish regulation insisted that there should be a 2-metr loadspace behind the driver's seat, that the loa floor should be completely level, and that ther should be no windows except in the tail door. A a result, Discovery Commercials shipped t Ireland between 1993 and 1994 had their Alpin lights blanked off, while a level floor was fixe into the rear. The necessary 2-metre space wa achieved by chopping off the rear of the centr console behind the gear-lever and moving th switches for the electric windows to a ne position in the console.

A radical solution also had to be found for th Dutch market, where Discoverys were able t qualify as commercials and therefore be exemp from taxation if certain criteria were met. Th Dutch authorities demanded a floor-to-ceilin height in the load area of at least 1.3 metre (52in), and that the rear side windows behin the driver had to be blacked-out. The roof had t be at least 25cm (9.84in) above the tops of th

In the Netherlands, three-door Discoverys were fitted with a higher roof by Ter Berg in order to qualify as commercial vehicles.

This Discovery was adapted for wheelchair transport during 1992 and featured a hydraulic tail-lift to enable the wheelchair and occupant to gain access through the rear door. At least two were built, the later one with a window in the sloping front of the roof.

This one was a home-built conversion dating from 1995, and turned an early three-door Discovery into a versatile five-seater pick-up.

The Discovery Commercial was based on the three-door model and was introduced during 1993.

side doors and there had to be a bulkhead at least 30cm (11.8in) high between the front seats and the load area in the rear.

A number of conversions had already been designed for some of the Japanese 4x4 vehicles sold in the Netherlands, all involving the addition of a raised roof to meet the loadspace

Discovery cabriolet a feasibility study for Freelander

area height criterion. Sales of these were strong enough to persuade the conversion specialists Ter Berg to develop a similar conversion for the Discovery, and this was sold through Land Rover dealers as an approved conversion.

The Ter Berg conversion was mostly applied to three-door models, although a few five-door

Discoverys were also converted. On the three-door model, the rear seats were removed and a 30cm bulkhead was added behind the front seats. The whole of the load area behind this was then lined, mostly with wood. The rear side windows were obscured with a dark grey film stuck on their inside surfaces. The major part of the conversion, however, was the creation of a completely new roof panel, several inches higher than standard, which retained the Discovery's characteristic Alpine lights – albeit obscured by the same dark film as was used on the side windows. This roof panel, not unlike the one created by LRSV for their wheelchair carrier, was made of steel and was welded to the bodyshell after the original panel had been cut off.

Known in Holland as a Hi-Roof Discovery, the Ter Berg conversion remained available until Dutch regulations changed at the end of 1994 and Land Rover introduced the standard Special Vehicles-built Discovery Commercial to the Netherlands. Several examples of the facelifted 1995 model-year Discovery were therefore converted, but most of the Ter Berg conversions were probably done on earlier 'Jay' Discoverys.

Looking very smart is this 1996 Discovery Commercial, again based on the three-door body, but incorporating all the improvements of the post-1994 mainstream models.

The Commercial offered a large load area and made for a very stylish van.

Land Rover looked at the idea of a Discovery cabriolet but rejected it, leaving the field clear for coachbuilders Vantagefield to produce this one for a Far Eastern client in 1993.

The Discovery cabriolet

LRSV also seem to have looked at the feasibility of a cabriolet version of the Discovery, and there is an unconfirmed story that two vehicles were made as feasibility studies. One was carried out by an outside coachbuilding firm, while the other was allegedly made by LRSV themselves. However, there seem to have been difficulties with the conversion, which would have made it an expensive one to offer. In view of the limited market potential – and perhaps also because work on 1997's three-door Freelander with its softback configuration was already under way – the idea was dropped.

Nevertheless, two Discovery cabriolets were built during 1993 as conversions by the custom specialists Vantagefield, of London. Both of these vehicles were specially-commissioned and were not related to the LRSV experiments – although it seems likely that LRSV did examine one of the Vantagefield vehicles at some point. One vehicle went to a customer in the Middle East, and the other – a green one – to a customer in Brunei.

CHAPTER 10

DISCOVERY IN ACTION

Off-road driving and events

Most people who buy a Discovery do so for its unique blend of style with a flexible and spacious interior. Perceived crashworthiness also comes into the equation – the Discovery is big and strong, and is therefore likely to protect its occupants in a collision. It is also undeniable that four-wheel-drive estates are fashionable, and have been since the early Eighties. However, relatively few people actually buy a Discovery for its off-road ability, and even those who do want to use it off-road have usually chosen it over other off-roaders because of its other qualities.

Obviously, no-one is going to buy an expensive and luxurious vehicle like this purely for its ability to slog through mud and over boulders. Yet it is a great pity that most owners will never come to appreciate just how good their vehicles are off the road. The Discovery is universally recognized as one of the great dual-purpose off-roaders (that is, one which is also at home on the road), and can offer its owner a great deal of leisure-time enjoyment if it is used sensibly off the road.

As prices of the earliest Discoverys have gradually come down, more and more people have started to use them for off-road entertainment. Perhaps this is as it should be: a vehicle used primarily for road work by its first two or three owners and then adopted as a weekend off-roader as well as weekday transport by subsequent owners is finally fulfilling its designers' aims.

However, there is very much more to off-roading than finding a stretch of land, selecting low ratio and going for it. Foremost among your considerations before driving off-road should be legal ones, such as whose land you are proposing to drive on and whether or not you are allowed to be there. Nothing spoils the enjoyment of responsible off-roaders quite as much as some idiot churning up privately-owned land without permission. The usual reaction is a letter or article in the local paper which condemns all off-roaders as an anti-social nuisance, and may cause formerly sympathetic landowners to withdraw permission for their land to be used.

Unfortunately, the regulations covering vehicular rights of way in the British countryside are complicated. If you cannot fight your way through them, your best bet is to consult the Rights of Way officer of your local off-road club (see Chapter 11). He or she will be able to tell you where you may go and when

Green Laning and the art of going softly

and, more important, where you may not take your vehicle. Do take notice of the advice you receive, and remember that the makers of your Discovery actively promote a responsible attitude to off-roading as part of their overall environmental policy. The views of Land Rover Ltd are contained in a booklet entitled *Fragile Earth*, which can be obtained through franchised dealerships. As this booklet points out, 'how little damage you do to the environment depends to a remarkable extent on how you drive. The golden rule is go softly. This will not only safeguard the environment, it will also help to protect you and your vehicle from

Gentle green laning does not tax a Discovery at all, but can be a rewarding pursuit.

sustaining serious damage.'

Straightforward off-road driving, where the objective is to enjoy the countryside rather than to challenge the vehicle, is known as Green Laning. There is no simple definition of a green lane, which is one reason the issues surrounding this pursuit are so complicated. You may drive off-road anywhere there is a vehicular Right of Way, but you must first establish that such a Right of Way does exist. Your local highway authority holds maps on which vehicular Rights of Way are marked, and you have a right to ask to see these maps. Your local County Council will probably have them marked as RUPPs (Roads Used as Public Paths), but the situation is further complicated because not all RUPPs have vehicular Rights of Way. You might also come across BOATs (Byways Open to All Traffic), which sound more promising until

you realize that here, too, a Traffic Regulation Order may restrict your right to drive along the BOAT.

Mostly, green laning will not damage your vehicle or even tax it greatly, and it is a very pleasant way of spending a summer afternoon. You will probably enjoy it most if you go in company with a couple of other vehicles, but please do not go in enormous convoys. That kind of thing gets off-roaders a bad name with walkers, horse-riders, farmers and casual onlookers alike.

If you want to indulge in the more testing forms of off-road motoring, you need to get rather better organized. The most sensible thing is to call on one of the many recognized off-road schools and learn something about how to tackle the more challenging situations there. As for the challenges themselves, which are really a

106

Specially-prepared off-road courses include obstacles like this 'bomb hole' – no problem for a Discovery.

Wading like this should only be undertaken after a recce on foot to check that there are no hidden underwater obstacles – or worse, even deeper holes!

form of motorsport conducted off-road, you will not find out about them unless you belong to one of the off-road clubs. Not all forms of off-road motorsport demand specially-prepared vehicles, and one of the most popular is the RTV (Road Taxed Vehicle) trial, in which roadgoing vehicles like yours can participate. You are unlikely to win unless you prepare your vehicle specially, but you can have a lot of fun just taking part.

The driver's handbook which comes with the Discovery offers a number of valuable hints on off-road driving, but it is worth elaborating on the subject here. Many people are tempted by the idea of off-roading, but are not quite sure what they might be letting themselves in for. If you are among them, what follows might help you to decide whether the activity is for you.

The most fundamental principle of off-road driving is to be prepared. Even in gentle green

107

The long-travel coil springs allow excellent axle articulation which in turn gives the best chance to retain traction in difficult going. This Discovery was pictured in the Australian outback.

laning, you should take some elementary precautions. It is going to be muddy out there, so wear wellington boots (you'd be surprised how many people don't – the first time). Take a shovel (in case the vehicle gets stuck), a strong towrope (in case it gets comprehensively stuck), and a First Aid Kit (because people hurt themselves at the most inconvenient moments, miles from civilization).

Being prepared also means knowing your vehicle. If you've never selected Low ratio or used the centre differential lock, make sure you know how to do so and that everything is working correctly before you go off-road. A manual Discovery has a total of 10 forward gears and two reverse (five forward and one reverse in High ratio and the same in Low). With an automatic model the choice is only slightly more restricted: there are eight forward gears and two reverse. Each one is best suited to certain conditions, and you should know which ones will best suit the sort of terrain you are likely to encounter.

You should also recognize the importance of tyres in off-road driving. Those supplied on your Discovery when it was new are a compromise design: they give good traction in most off-road conditions, and on metalled roads they run quietly and are strong enough to cope with two

tons of Discovery being flung around bends at 90mph. However, they are not the ultimate in off-road tyres by any means, and for really difficult terrain you should fit one of the specialist types of off-road tyre. Only dedicated off-roaders do so, as these tyres are generally not very good on the road. For further advice on this subject, consult one of the specialist magazines, like *Land Rover Monthly, Land Rover Owner, Land Rover World* or *Off-Road & 4 Wheel Drive.*

In off-road conditions, the occupants of any vehicle tend to get thrown about quite a lot. This is why the Discovery has grab-handles above each of the passenger doors and (on 1989-94 models) an additional passenger grab-rail on the dashboard. The driver makes do without because he has the steering wheel to hang on to; but it is vital not to hang on to that wheel too tightly off-road. As the front wheels hit bumps, rocks and potholes, even the steering damper will be unable to prevent the steering wheel from being jerked quite violently. In particular, don't hook your thumbs around the rim of the wheel, because one of these jerks could easily spin the wheel hard enough for one of the spokes to break your thumb. Those bumps also mean that you should not rest your foot on the clutch of a manual-transmission Discovery

Some types of off-roading do demand special equipment, such as winches. Lightweight alloy ladders allow this Discovery to be driven across a deep hollow which would otherwise have been impassable.

because a serious jolt could cause you to declutch involuntarily and so lose traction just at the wrong moment. It is also a good idea to wear seat belts off-road.

Many people are surprised to find that off-roading is not all about rushing at obstacles like a bull in a china shop. In fact, all off-road driving is done slowly (except for some competitive events where the course has been checked in advance). Even so, you will not always have to use the Low ratios. On firm, level ground (such as forest tracks), High ratios will usually do the trick as long as you keep your speed down. However, if there is any risk that the wheels will spin, you should engage the centre differential lock to maintain traction. The Low ratios will give greater traction for soft ground, and they also give greater control if you have to inch your vehicle carefully over or past an obstacle. Naturally, the Low gears will restrict your speed considerably.

Newcomers to off-roading often make the mistake of selecting too low a gear for the conditions. The result is usually wheelspin, which will cause the vehicle to lose traction and dig itself into soft ground. Second gear Low or third gear Low are usually all you will need, even on hilly terrain. First gear Low is best reserved for steep descents. In such

circumstances, novice off-roaders are usually tempted to use the brakes to control the descent. In fact, the V8 petrol and Tdi diesel engines in the Discovery have sufficient engine braking (the engine's ability to hold the vehicle back or slow it down) to make controlled descents without assistance from either the accelerator or the brake pedal. You won't believe that until you try it for yourself, though!

Off-road driving techniques are easy to learn

Crossing ditches and driving in the tracks of other vehicles both call for special techniques, which are nevertheless quite straightforward and easy to learn. The Discovery handbook provides enough instruction on these for the novice to learn very quickly. As with anything else in off-road driving, however, it is vital not to rush into things. Try out the techniques slowly

109

until you are sure you know what you are doing. Lastly, never attempt to cross an obstacle 'blind'. Stop and get out of the vehicle to see what lies ahead (or get a sensible passenger to do it for you), then think about what to do and take it gently.

Steering and braking off-road also call for special techniques. Don't expect the vehicle to respond to sudden steering inputs in the same way as it does on the road. You need to turn the wheel gently and purposefully; sudden changes of lock will probably result in the vehicle carrying straight on with the front wheels sliding sideways at an angle. In a worst case, the sliding wheels may regain traction suddenly and pull you off-course into an obstacle. Remember that it is often difficult in off-road driving to be certain which way the front wheels are pointing. If in doubt, stop as soon as you sensibly can, get out and have a look.

Use the brakes sparingly off-road because braking can cause the wheels to lock while momentum carries the vehicle along. In such circumstances, you will have no traction and will therefore have lost control of the vehicle. Wherever possible, therefore, use the gears to slow the vehicle down. The ABS brakes on later Discoverys will reduce the chances of a slide off-road, but it is still safer to think of them as for emergencies only. They cannot overcome the laws of physics!

You do not need a winch for self-recovery off-road unless you intend to tackle some particularly difficult terrain where the vehicle is likely to get stuck. Conversely, of course, don't try to cross difficult ground where you think you might get stuck unless your Discovery is fitted with a winch, or you have a colleague on hand with another vehicle and a towrope. Many farmers find it very funny to see a young idiot stuck in the mud in his shiny new four-wheel-drive vehicle, and some will ask for a contribution to expenses before getting the tractor out to pull you clear.

The more you understand the art of off-road driving, the more you will enjoy it and the more pleasure you will be able to get from your Discovery. There is nothing quite like the characteristic smells of off-roading, such as mud baking on a hot exhaust pipe, and nothing quite like the exhilaration of crossing a difficult piece of terrain by careful co-operation between driver and vehicle.

Camel Trophy
At a level way beyond the gentle green laning

Off-road driving is taught at a number of professional establishments, and among them is Land Rover's own driving school, the Land Rover Experience. Note that this is a top-specification Discovery ES!

The new Discovery introduced in 1998 was every bit as capable off-road as the old. This XS model is fording a shallow stream in the Scottish Highlands.

afternoons and club RTV trials are competitive international off-road events. These include long-distance marathons like the annual Paris-Dakar Rally, which demands very special vehicles. Mostly, the winning machines are very heavily modified versions of production types, backed by vast sums of their manufacturers' money. Land Rover has elected to steer well clear of such events, although Land Rover France has supported teams entering Discoverys in a limited number of endurance competitions.

Nevertheless, between 1981 and 1998, Land Rover put a great deal of money into the Camel Trophy, which is less of a race than a combination of adventure and expedition. The Camel Trophy was conceived in West Germany in the late Seventies, and the first event was held in the Amazon basin in 1980, with the backing of R J Reynolds Tobacco GmbH, the manufacturers of Camel cigarettes. The following year, Land Rover became involved, and every year up to 1998 the company provided the vehicles for the Trophy, which it saw as offering superb worldwide publicity. As Land Rover's sales and marketing director John Russell told *Land Rover Owner* magazine after the 1990 event, the first to use Discoverys: 'We saw the Camel Trophy as the ideal opportunity to prove that our newcomer was just as tough and

reliable as its stablemates. The fact that, after 1,500km of off-roading in Siberia, 98 per cent of the spares we provided remained unused, is testimony to Discovery's strength and durability.'

After that first outing in 1990, Discoverys were used on every Camel Trophy up to and including the 1997 event, after which the publicity switched to the new Freelander. The nature of the Trophy, however, had changed quite dramatically by that time. After something approaching a fiasco on the 1996 Trophy, which had to be curtailed when appalling weather conditions made progress too difficult, the focus switched from the vehicle-borne expedition side to special events designed to test the mettle of the competitors, and the abilities of the vehicles were rather less important in 1997 than they had been earlier. Arguably, the Discovery had more than made its mark as the archetypal Camel Trophy crew vehicle, and in some quarters the continuing relevance of the event was already being questioned by this stage.

Between 1990 and 1996, the Camel Trophy was best described as a combination of expedition and challenge, in which teams from many different countries negotiated tracks and trails through jungle and other exotic but difficult terrain in a loose convoy. The aim was

A three-door Discovery splashes through a river on the 1990 Camel Trophy in Siberia. There is no need to throw water this high – the shot was staged for the camera.

to get all the vehicles and teams through, and to that end, the competing teams actually helped one another instead of trying to do one another down.

The event was always divided into two sections, an expedition section and a special tasks section, and the winners of the Camel Trophy itself were the team who had been most successful in both of these. The special tasks – actually run at intervals along the main expedition route – ranged from simple winching exercises through night navigation to difficult

Camel Trophy success leads to limited editions

river crossings, and all had to be carried out using only the equipment carried on the vehicle. But the Camel Trophy was not the only prize on the event which bore its name: there was also a Team Spirit Award, gained during the expedition section, which went to the team which made the greatest contribution to the overall success and achievement of the event.

All Camel Trophy events have taken place with the full approval of the Governments whose territories they have used, and at the heart of the Trophy's philosophy has always been

a fundamental respect for the environment through which it has travelled. It has always been one of the Camel Trophy's aims to promote sensitive use of the environment, and to that end it did not drive through virgin jungle or cut down trees and foliage willy-nilly *en route*. Wherever possible, it used existing roads and trails, often repairing roads and bridges along the way by using timber which had already fallen or had been provided by the local authority. And the support team of mechanics, medics and others has often lent aid to local communities as the Camel Trophy passed through.

That the Camel Trophy had publicity value in some countries was undeniable, and the interest which the event generates was met in Germany and Japan with special limited-edition Camel Trophy Discoverys. In addition, there is a healthy demand worldwide for vehicles which were used on Trophy events, even though some of them had to be quite extensively rebuilt before being sold on by Land Rover!

All the Camel Trophy Discoverys were five-door turbodiesels except those used on the 1990 event, which were three-door turbodiesel models. Basically standard production-line vehicles, all of them were nevertheless specially equipped by Land Rover Special Vehicles or by its SVO predecessor. Thus, for example, they had special Michelin XCL tyres on rugged steel (rather than alloy) wheels, auxiliary lighting, bull-bars and light guards, a powerful winch, a rollcage and a roof rack for carrying additional equipment. All of them were painted in the distinctive Sandglow colour associated with the Camel Trophy (which

Teamwork: Camel Trophy crews get together to rescue a stranded Discovery on the 1995 Mundo Maya event.

It takes a skilled driver to negotiate a log bridge like this one, constructed by the Camel Trophy crews on the 1996 Kalimantan event.

The vehicles used on the Camel Trophy are often sold on to the public and have their own enthusiasts' club. This five-door Discovery was used by the Dutch team on the 1991 Tanzania-Burundi event and is now in private hands. *(Picture by courtesy of Ian Gough.)*

is actually an old Austin-Morris car colour), and all of them had the national flag and names of the crew members painted on each front wing. No vehicle was ever used on more than one Camel Trophy, although the previous year's vehicles were often used in training and selection trials for a forthcoming event.

The Camel Trophy events involving the Discovery are listed below. The Discoverys were always used by the competing crews; the support vehicles were invariably Land Rover utilities.

1990 – Siberia/USSR
16 competing nations using 16 200Tdi three-door Discoverys; Camel Trophy won by the Netherlands

1991- Tanzania-Burundi
17 competing nations using 17 200Tdi five-door Discoverys; Camel Trophy won by Turkey

1992- Guyana
16 competing nations using 16 200Tdi five-door Discoverys; Camel Trophy won by Switzerland

1993 – Sabah, Malaysia
16 competing nations using 16 200Tdi five-door Discoverys; Camel Trophy won by the USA

1994 – Argentina-Paraguay-Chile
18 competing nations using 18 200Tdi five-door Discoverys; Camel Trophy won by Spain

1995 – Mundo Maya
20 competing nations using 20 300Tdi five-door Discoverys; Camel Trophy won by Czechoslovakia

1996 – Kalimantan
20 competing nations using 20 300Tdi five-door Discoverys; Camel Trophy won by Greece

1997 – Mongolia
20 competing nations using 20 300Tdi five-door Discoverys; Camel Trophy won by Austria

CHAPTER 11

YOUR OWN DISCOVERY

Buying and owning

Car buying is rarely an entirely rational business, and the rational element is likely to be glaringly absent when it comes to buying a vehicle with the fashionable appeal of a Discovery. Many people approach the purchase of such a vehicle with little more than a burning ambition to have one, and in that state of excitement they are more than likely to make an expensive mistake.

The sensible thing to do in such circumstances is to take a step backwards mentally and work out exactly why you want a Discovery. You need to go beyond the obvious answers – 'because it looks good', 'because all my friends have got one', or 'because it will complement my lifestyle and image' – and think exactly what you are going to expect of it. If you then base your choice of vehicle on that knowledge, you will not be disappointed.

What exactly do you want?

The Discovery is a first-rate off-roader, but not every Discovery buyer intends to take it off-road. There is no shame in admitting that you might never use the vehicle off-road at all. You will be in good company because the vast majority of Discovery owners rarely if ever use their vehicles' off-road abilities.

On the other hand, if off-roading is one of the major reasons why you plan to buy a Discovery, you need a V8, V8i, Tdi or Td5 model as these have the low-down grunt which is necessary in off-road motoring. An Mpi would be a good choice if you just expect to do some occasional green laning, but it is rather less able when the going gets tough. If your Discovery will be used for serious off-road work, there is really no point in paying the extra to get five doors, seven seats, or a collection of luxury equipment. Go for the least well-equipped vehicle you can find (as long

as it is sound in other ways); it will save you money and will be just as capable off-road as any of the others.

Next consider how many people you plan to carry in the vehicle. If you are single and are unlikely to carry more than a couple of extra friends at any one time, a three-door Discovery with the standard five-seat configuration will be perfectly adequate. It should also cost you less than an equivalent five-door model. However, if you have a family to carry around, you really should think in terms of a five-door model. Children might like to scramble over the tipped front seats and into the rear, but the

---

Size matters
when carrying
the family

---

arrangement is hardly convenient, especially if you are in a hurry. Similarly, elderly or infirm relatives will not take kindly to getting into the back seat of a three-door model, so think of their needs if you regularly carry such passengers. You might even consider fitting running-boards to help them get in and out of a vehicle which sits much higher off the ground than a conventional car.

If you have a large family, or regularly carry a lot of friends around, you might need the seven-seat option, with its two additional seats in the rear. Children love these seats – but parents in the front seats will have difficulty in hearing

Quality control was not always a strong point in the Discovery. The variation in the door gap is clear in this picture of a 1995 model, taken when it was brand new.

them when the vehicle is running at speed. Also remember that the two rear seats are not really comfortable for anyone over about 5 feet 8 inches tall, and luggage space inside the vehicle is severely restricted when they are occupied. An option on the latest 'Tempest' Discovery is a pair of headphones with their own volume controls for occupants of the two occasional seats – very handy for those with children whose musical tastes differ from their own! These latest Discoverys also have forward-facing rather than inward-facing seats, and legroom is even more restricted.

It is also vital to make the right choice of engine, and there are several considerations here. All the petrol-engined models depreciate faster than the turbodiesel equivalents, so they will be cheaper to buy secondhand. However, the turbodiesel Discoverys have always sold in far larger numbers – typically about four to one in countries where both types have been available – so there may not be a very wide choice of petrol-engined models on offer. Of the petrol-engined types, the Mpi models, which were never numerous, are still not very popular as secondhand buys. They may be cheap, therefore, but there will not be many for sale.

An important reason for the popularity of the turbodiesel models is their excellent fuel economy. Both Tdi and Td5 types can be expected to return around 25-35mpg in everyday use, which compares very favourably with the 22-24mpg of an Mpi and the 17-18mpg of a fuel-injected V8. The early carburettor V8s

High mileages take their toll on the early seats, whose coverings began to wear through and fray. The steering wheel also goes shiny . . .

. . . as does the knob of the main gear-lever.

Listen for top-end rattle and look for oil leaks on the V8 engines. Injected engines, like this 3.9-litre type, suffer from all kinds of problems if the ECU malfunctions.

can be frighteningly thirsty, and figures of 14-15mpg are quite normal. Turbodiesels need more frequent service attention – an oil change every 6,000 miles as opposed to the 12,000 miles recommended for the petrol types. However, long-term owners of V8 models also swear by 6,000-mile oil changes in order to keep their engines in good health, especially as the miles mount up.

If you must have on-road performance, the 3.9-litre or 4.0-litre V8i models are the best bet. All the V8 models offer greater levels of refinement (lower noise, smoother pulling power) than the Mpi and Tdi, but it is questionable whether their refinement is greater than that of the Td5 turbodiesel. For all-round ability, it is hard to fault the Tdi, which offers extremely good fuel economy for a vehicle of the Discovery's size and weight, together with reasonable road performance and acceptable refinement. The later 300Tdi (1994-98) is much quieter and smoother than the early 200Tdi (1989-94), which may have been a revelation when it was new but sounds harsh and raucous by the standards of more modern diesels. As for the Td5 engine (1998 on), refinement, performance and fuel economy are all outstanding, and this is undoubtedly the one to go for if your budget will stretch that far.

Many people buy four-wheel-drive vehicles like the Discovery because of their suitability for towing. If this is one of your main reasons for buying a Discovery, you will undoubtedly be better off with either a turbodiesel or a V8 model. Avoid the Mpi, except for light-duty towing: it is very much less able than the other models because of its relative lack of low-down torque. This was improved to some extent on post-1994 models, but not enough to make the Mpi acceptable for heavy-duty work.

It is worth mentioning here that there has never been any shortage of aftermarket modifications for the Discovery's power units. The V8 engine has been around in Rover products since 1967, and in the early 1960s it was used in a number of 'compact' American cars built by the Buick, Oldsmobile and Pontiac divisions of General Motors. All this means that a wealth of tuning expertise is available. There are plenty of performance modification kits which involve nothing more than camshaft and carburettor changes (or reprogramming of the ECU on fuel-injected engines), or for more major work there have been turbochargers, superchargers and capacity enlargements up to as much as 5 litres. The highly-regarded Overfinch company even offers replacement 5.7-litre engines of General Motors origin, which give huge performance improvements without detriment to off-road or towing ability.

As for the Tdi types, Rover's own Director of Powertrain Engineering has admitted that as

Performance upgrades have always been available. This Sprintex supercharger was available for the early carburetted Discovery engine from Dennis Priddle Racing.

much as 140bhp or so can be extracted reliably from them. Several specialist companies offer modifications which boost power to around 132bhp and torque to around 235lb.ft, and at least one modification has claimed 170bhp, although in that case the maximum turbocharger boost had to be used only for short periods to avoid damage to the engine. If noise levels are a problem, there are several soundproofing kits which will reduce the

Warranty claims highlight urgent need for change

amount of diesel rattle transmitted to the passenger cabin.

The Mpi is a rather different matter. It is true that other versions of the engine provide as much as 197bhp, and that some Italian companies have offered performance improvements through turbocharger conversions. However, on the whole there is little aftermarket expertise on this engine. Its

biggest problem – not always addressed by aftermarket upgrades – is its poor bottom-end torque, and it is probably more cost-effective to replace the engine with a V8 or a turbodiesel than to try tuning the existing engine.

What goes wrong?

Fundamentally, the Discovery is a robust, reliable vehicle. However, it has been afflicted by poor build quality, which at some periods became simply intolerable. The worst years for build quality problems were 1995 and 1996, when production volumes increased to levels beyond those which Land Rover had ever anticipated. When asked for his opinion of the poor quality which afflicted Land Rover's best-selling vehicle at the time, the Chairman of the BMW Group which owned the company was unequivocal in his condemnation. 'It is a disgrace and has to be changed immediately,' he said.

Mostly, the problems, even in those bad years, were niggling faults which were sorted out under warranty. Nevertheless, a number of rogue vehicles suffered from a succession of irritating problems, one after the other. Land Rover dealers tore their hair out over the amount of warranty work they had to do, and in a number of cases ended up with an unforgivable couldn't-care-less attitude which was well documented in the specialist press at

Too much noise from a Tdi diesel? Aftermarket sound-deadening kits are the answer. This is part of the kit offered by Warwick Banks Handling.

The VIN of a Discovery is stamped into this plate on the bonnet lock platform. Make sure it matches the number on the registration document!

the time. Fortunately, those days seem to be over.

When buying a Discovery of any age, check the **engine** as the first stage in your mechanical inspection. The most popular Tdi engines may sound rattly, especially in earlier 200Tdi form, but they do not often give trouble. Heavy vibration can sometimes lead to looseness in pipe unions, and is worth investigating further: is an engine mounting on the way out (not common), or is something more serious amiss? The 6,000-mile oil change *must* be carried out without fail if the engine is to maintain its

health, so you should always check the service record of a Tdi engine, then double-check the level and condition of the oil. Black and treacly oil means trouble, and the turbocharger in particular is sensitive to dirty oil. Bear in mind the notorious difficulty of obtaining the same reading twice in succession on the Tdi engine's long and tortuous dipstick! It is also important to carry out a smoke check. After allowing the engine to idle for a while, stab the accelerator pedal and have an assistant watch the exhaust. Black smoke demands further investigation: there may be injector problems, or there may be piston ring and bore wear.

The V8s should be smooth and quiet at all times. Rattling noises from the top end indicate valvetrain problems. A light rustling sound could suggest a sticking hydraulic tappet, which can often be rectified simply by cleaning out the oilways with flushing oil. Heavier rapping sounds, however, probably mean there is wear in the camshaft. If so, the reason is probably that oil changes have not been carried out as regularly as they should be – so expect other signs of neglect elsewhere. Oil leaks are not uncommon on these engines, and can be troublesome to cure.

Poor performance from an early carburettor V8 usually suggests nothing more expensive than a tune-up is called for, but similar trouble on an injected engine may be more serious. The commonest cause of trouble is the ECU 'black box' which controls the ignition and fuelling. Erratic idling, stalling and other maladies are all usually traceable to an ECU fault. Unfortunately, DIY solutions do not exist: the ECU has to be replaced, and it is quite expensive.

The Mpi engines are typical of four-valve types in their thrashiness and harshness at high revs. At normal driving speeds they should be relatively refined and sound much like a modern saloon car engine. Loss of refinement suggests valvetrain problems, and of course there is an ECU to suspect if there are problems with idling, cutting out, flat spots and the like.

The next mechanical component to check is the **gearbox**, of which there have been two types of five-speed manual and two types of four-speed automatic. On models built up to 1994, the five-speed type is the LT77, which gained improved synchromesh on the lower gears in 1991 to become the LT77S. Later five-speed gearboxes are the R380. All automatic gearboxes have been made by ZF and are the 4HP22 variety; from 1998, however, an electro-hydraulic control system was added, which allowed a switchable 'Sport' mode. The automatic gearboxes are troublefree in normal use, so any difficulties here need careful investigation.

The LT77 and LT77S gearboxes are fairly

Some tell-tale signs of possible transmission troubles

trouble-free, although the earlier type may be very difficult to get into first gear when cold. The cure for this was to use automatic transmission fluid in place of the standard gearbox oil. A rattle in neutral suggests worn layshaft bearings, and a judder in third suggests the oil level is low: oil leaks are quite common. The R380 gearbox has a much slicker gearchange action and is generally much better. However, during the poor build quality period of 1995-96, this component probably gave more

The bottle jack and wheel chock are stored under the bonnet, but the jack handle and wheelbrace are under the back seat. Check that they are all present on a vehicle offered for sale.

trouble than any other. As often as not, the gearbox would simply lock up, so that it was impossible to select or change from any gear. Problem cases should all have been sorted out under warranty by now, but there may be some trouble still waiting for the unwary.

Five-speed models usually produce an assortment of clunks from the drivetrain on the over-run and when the drive is taken up. This is quite normal, and is a result of the number of universal joints in the driveline, all of which allow a certain amount of play. Driveline 'shunt' is also present on automatics, although the torque converter tends to cushion this. The post-1998 models have ASC (Anti-Shunt Control) which overcomes this problem electronically by smoothing out sudden increases or decreases in power.

The **transfer gearbox** in all Discovery models is the LT230 gear-driven type. In early models it emits a pronounced whine, which is quite normal if rather irritating. Later versions are quieter, and gear whine is non-existent on 1998 and later models. The louder the noise, the

Wheel changes involve use of differential lock

greater the chance there is wear in the gearbox. Check that there is no damage to the Low-range gears (heavy off-road work can chip teeth on the gearwheels), by selecting Low range and driving a few yards. The noise of damaged gear teeth is unmistakable.

Even if you have no intention of doing any off-roading, you must ensure that the centre differential lock is working because you need to use it for changing a wheel. Do not expect the dashboard warning light to come on immediately, but drive forward a small distance after selecting the lock to ensure that it has engaged. As a double-check, try putting the steering on full lock and driving a short distance. If the differential lock is working, you will feel a judder down the driveline. Post-1998 models have no differential lock, but you should still check that Low ratio can be successfully engaged. If not, something has seized!

There are unlikely to be any problems with the **chassis** unless the vehicle has been involved in a serious accident or has done a lot of hard off-road work. Discovery chassis are well-

protected from new against rust, but repair work might not have been followed by re-protection – so take a look. Beware, too, of a vehicle which has been used for launching a boat, because the salt water into which it will have been driven can accelerate corrosion at the rear of the chassis. Cross-members can be dented by collisions with rocks off-road, but this should not be a cause for real worry unless the damage is severe or is causing something to foul. However, even minor damage can be a reason for negotiation on the asking price!

Steering, suspension and brakes do not present major problems, either. However, you should watch for fluid leaks from the power-assisted steering, particularly from the steering box itself. If the Discovery seems to sit down low at the back, it may have tired rear springs caused by regular overloading or heavy towing. Check, too, that the vehicle sits all-square, as a pronounced lean to one quarter suggests there might be spring trouble, which deserves further investigation. Cornering roll at speed is to be expected, especially on early models without anti-roll bars. Roll is much less noticeable when the bars are fitted (and retro-fitting is possible with a kit from Land Rover Parts). For true freedom from cornering roll, however, the ACE system introduced in 1998 reigns supreme.

All versions of the Discovery depend on rubber bushing in the suspension, and inevitably these bushes wear over time. Worn bushes on the front and rear radius arms show up as imprecise handling, but are not very expensive to replace. The pre-1998 models also have an A-frame which locates the rear axle, and this is attached to the chassis-frame by a ball-joint which can also wear. A worn ball-joint here makes a distinctive knocking noise when the vehicle is moving.

Brakes are powerful and should pull the vehicle up squarely. When testing, however, do not try to stop the vehicle with the handbrake as you might on a conventional car. The Discovery's handbrake does not operate on the rear wheels but on the transmission, and applying it while the vehicle is in motion could cause expensive damage. Do not worry if the vehicle rolls downhill slightly if you apply the handbrake on a hill. The movement will be no more than a few inches and is caused by the slack in the transmission, which has to be taken up before the braked transmission can also prevent the wheels from turning.

Worth a second look are the **wheels**, especially the popular alloy types. The styled steel wheels do not normally present problems, and if they start to look scruffy in their old age they can usually be restored with a rub-down and a coat of silver paint. The alloys, however, can become

An important consideration in buying a Discovery may be the vehicle's height. It stands 6ft 3.5in (192cm) off the ground, which makes it a tight fit in many domestic garages and denies it entry to some multi-storey car parks.

Side steps can make access to the vehicle easier for elderly passengers.

damaged from kerbing, or by tyre fitters who use clip-on weights instead of the stick-on type specially designed for alloy wheels. Once their protective coating has been damaged they will start to corrode – and few things look worse than a stylish alloy wheel which has started to deteriorate. All types should be fairly easy to replace with new, but you should remember that alloy wheels are expensive. Some specialist companies will restore damaged alloy wheels, so it is worth comparing costs before buying new replacements.

The **body** is generally very strong, although panel gaps are often larger than ideal and can be uneven. Build quality problems in the mid-1990s led to leaks through the windscreen and Alpine light seals, which may still be present. If so, it means they have proved hard to cure! The

---

Watch out for aluminium and steel corrosion

---

usual tell-tale is water marks on the trim around the affected area.

Aluminium corrosion is gradually becoming a problem as the vehicles get older, just as it always has been on Land Rover utilities and Range Rovers with aluminium alloy panels. The most vulnerable areas are the bottoms of the doors, the tailgate and around the lower body at the rear. The steel elements rust, too, and this is particularly noticeable on bumpers and roof rails where the protective finish has chipped off.

Other body problems have been associated with the tail door, and early models had weak hinges, which should have been replaced under warranty. On all models you should check the tail door lock for correct functioning, and make sure that it locks and unlocks correctly if it is wired into the central locking system (as it should be on most Discoverys). On early three-door models there were also some weaknesses in the fittings of the rear side windows. Vehicles which have been used off-road are likely to

suffer from damage to the lower panels, and in particular to the plastic side sills, so it is worth checking carefully in these areas.

The **interior** is generally hard-wearing, but the pre-1994 seat coverings are now demonstrating a tendency to wear through and fray. The early steering wheel and gear-lever also become shiny after high mileages, and this seems to show up more on Discoverys with the original Sonar Blue interior trim. Leather trim is durable, but it does need periodic treatment with hide food if it is to remain supple and not dry out and crack. On vehicles fitted with electric windows and door mirrors, you should check that everything works properly, because electric motors can fail.

Lastly, always remember to check the vehicle's **documentation** when buying. High demand and the relative ease of breaking into a Discovery ensured that a lot of vehicles were stolen in the early days before decent immobilization systems were fitted. Many were never recovered, and it is a fair bet that a good number were 'ringed' – given the identity of another vehicle – and sold on. The bolt-together nature of the pre-1998 Discovery also means that some vehicles will have been created from the parts of two or more others which may have been written off after crash damage. Some 'Discoverys' have even been created by fitting a Discovery body onto a Range Rover chassis and drivetrain. If in doubt over any of these issues, make sure that the numbers on the vehicle match those on the registration documents, and check the component numbers against those in Appendix B.

Like all vehicles which inspire more than the usual amount of devotion in their owners, the Discovery has its own club. Club Discovery is a small but growing organization which offers members special days out and discounts on certain products available from Warwick Banks Handling, from whose premises it operates. Club Discovery can be contacted at West Farm, Witham-on-the-Hill, Bourne, Lincolnshire PE10 0JN.

Several other clubs welcome Discovery owners, and most of these are organized primarily to promote off-road or camping and caravanning activities. A full list of the Land Rover clubs is published regularly in *Land Rover Owner* and in some of the other off-road magazines.

APPENDIX A
TECHNICAL SPECIFICATIONS

Note: The specifications given relate to UK-market models. Dates are for calendar-year and also relate to UK-market models only. Exceptions are indicated in the tables.

Discovery, 1989-1994 (Jay)
Engines:

(i) *(Tdi models)* '200 Tdi' 2,495cc 4-cylinder OHV direct-injection diesel, with turbocharger and intercooler. 90.47mm bore x 97mm stroke. Iron block and alloy cylinder head; five main bearings; belt-driven camshaft. Compression ratio 19.5:1. Maximum power 111.3bhp (83Kw) at 4,000rpm; maximum torque 195lb.ft (265Nm) at 1,800rpm.

(ii) *(V8 models, 1989-1990)* 3,528cc V8-cylinder OHV petrol, with twin SU carburettors. 88.9mm bore x 71.12mm stroke. Alloy block and cylinder heads; five main bearings; chain-driven camshaft. Compression ratio 8.13:1. Maximum power 144.5bhp (107.75Kw) at 5,000rpm; maximum torque 192lb.ft (260Nm) at 2,800rpm. Optional exhaust catalyst and lower-powered engine.

(iii) *(V8i models, 1990-1993)* 3,528cc V8-cylinder OHV petrol, with Lucas-Bosch fuel injection. 88.9mm bore x 71.12mm stroke. Alloy block and cylinder heads; five main bearings; chain-driven camshaft. Compression ratio 9.35:1, or 8.13:1 when equipped with exhaust catalyst. Non-cat engines: maximum power 163.6bhp (122Kw) at 4,750rpm; maximum torque 211.9lb.ft (288Nm) at 3,000rpm. Engines with exhaust catalyst: 153.4bhp (115Kw) at 4,750rpm and 192.1lb.ft (260Nm) at 3,000rpm.

(iv) *(V8i models, 1993-1994)* 3,947cc V8-cylinder OHV petrol, with Lucas-Bosch fuel injection. 93.98mm bore x 71.12mm stroke. Alloy block and cylinder heads; five main bearings; chain-driven camshaft. Compression ratio 9.35:1. Exhaust catalyst standard. Maximum power 180bhp (134Kw) at 4,750rpm; maximum torque 230lb.ft (312Nm) at 3,100rpm.

(v) *(Mpi models, 1993-1994)* 1,994cc 4-cylinder DOHC four-valve petrol, with MEMS 1.6 engine management controlling multi-point fuel injection. 84.45mm bore x 89mm stroke. Iron block and alloy cylinder head; five main bearings; belt-driven camshafts. Compression ratio 10:1. Exhaust catalyst standard. Maximum power 134bhp (100Kw) at 6,000rpm; maximum torque 137lb.ft (186Nm) at 2,500rpm.

Transmission:
Permanent four-wheel drive with lockable centre differential.
Five-speed all-synchromesh LT77 manual gearbox (LT77S from 1991) with hydraulically-operated 10.5-inch single-dry-plate clutch; gear ratios 3.692:1, 2.132:1, 1.397:1, 1.00:1, 0.77:1 (0.791:1 on Mpi models), reverse 3.429:1.
Optional ZF 4HP22 automatic gearbox (1992-1994 on V8i models, 1993-1994 on Tdi models, not available on Mpi models); gear ratios 2.48:1, 1.48:1, 1.00:1, 0.728:1, reverse 2.086:1.
Two-speed LT230T transfer gearbox; gear ratios 1.222:1 (High range) and 3.320:1 (Low range).
Front and rear final drive ratios 3.538:1.

Steering, suspension and brakes:
Power-assisted worm-and-roller steering with 3.375 turns lock to lock.
Live front axle with linear-rate coil springs and hydraulic telescopic dampers, located by radius arms and Panhard rod. Live rear axle with progressive-rate coil springs and hydraulic telescopic dampers, located by radius arms and A-frame. Front and rear anti-roll bars optional in Freestyle Choice package from 1993.
Disc brakes on all four wheels with 11.77in (299mm) diameter discs at the front and 11.42in (290mm) discs at the rear; vacuum servo assistance; dual hydraulic circuit on front wheels. Internal expanding drum-type parking brake operating on transfer box output shaft.
16-inch wheels with 205 R 16 tyres, or 235/70 R 16 tyres in Freestyle Choice package from 1993.

Dimensions:

Wheelbase	100in (2,540mm)
Front track	58.5in (1,486mm)
Rear track	58.5in (1,486mm)
Length	178in (4,521mm)
Width	70.6in (1,793mm) over door mirrors
Height	75.6in (1,920mm) without roof bars; 77.5in (1,968mm) with roof bars
Ground clearance	8.1in (204mm)
Kerb weight	4,359lb (3-dr V8), 4,432lb (3-dr Tdi), 4,363lb (3-dr V8i)

Discovery, 1994-1998 (Romulus)
Engines:

(i) *(Tdi models)* '300Tdi' 2,495cc 4-cylinder intercooled turbodiesel; main details unchanged from earlier 200Tdi engine.

(ii) *(V8i models)* 3,947cc V8-cylinder petrol. Details as on 1993-1994 engines except maximum power now 181.8bhp (135.5Kw) at 4,750rpm, and maximum torque 231lb.ft (314Nm) at 3,100rpm.

(iii) *(Mpi models)* 1,994cc 4-cylinder petrol. Details as on 1993-1994 engines except maximum torque now 140lb.ft (190Nm) at 3,600rpm.

Transmission:
As on 1989-1994 models except:
Five-speed all-synchromesh R380 gearbox with hydraulically-operated 10.5-inch single-dry-plate clutch; gear ratios 3.321:1, 2.132:1, 1.397:1, 1.00:1, fifth gear 0.770:1 (Tdi models), 0.730:1 (V8i models) or 0.791:1 (Mpi models), reverse 3.429:1.
Optional ZF 4HP22 automatic gearbox (Tdi and V8i models only); gear ratios as before.
Two-speed LT230T transfer gearbox; gear ratios 1.222:1 (High range) and 3.320:1 (Low range) on Tdi and V8i, or 1.41:1 (High range) and 3.761:1 (Low range) on Mpi.

Steering, suspension and brakes:
As on 1989-1994 models except front and rear anti-roll bars now standard; 11.73in (298mm) ventilated

front disc brakes; ABS brakes standard on ES-specification models and optional on others; Freestyle package now consists of alloy wheels with 235/70 R 16 tyres only.

Dimensions:
As on 1989-1994 models except overall length now 178.6in (4,538mm) and kerb weights as follows: 4,158lb (3-dr Mpi); 4,231lb (3-dr 3.9 V8i); 4,235lb (5-dr Mpi); 4,379lb (5-dr 3.9 V8i S); 4,527lb (5-dr Tdi S).

Discovery, 1998 on (Tempest)
Engines:
   (i)   *(Td5 models)* 'Storm' 2,495cc 5-cylinder OHC diesel, with electronic unit injectors, turbocharger and intercooler. 84.5mm bore x 89.0mm stroke. Iron block and alloy cylinder head; five main bearings; chain-driven camshaft. Compression ratio 19.5:1. Maximum power 136bhp (101.5Kw) at 4,200rpm; maximum torque 221lb.ft (300Nm) at 1,950rpm with manual gearbox or 232lb.ft (315Nm) with automatic transmission.
   (ii) *(V8i models)* 'Thor' 3,947cc V8-cylinder OHV petrol, with Bosch 5.2.1 fuel and ignition management system. 93.98mm bore x 71.12mm stroke. Alloy block and cylinder heads; five main bearings; chain-driven camshaft. Compression ratio 9.35:1. Exhaust catalyst standard. Maximum power 182bhp (136Kw) at 4,750rpm; maximum torque 250lb.ft (340Nm) at 2,600rpm.

Transmission:
Permanent four-wheel drive with electronic traction control system.
Five-speed all-synchromesh R380 manual gearbox with hydraulically-operated 10.5-inch single-dry-plate clutch; gear ratios 3.692:1 (3.321:1 on V8i models), 2.132:1, 1.397:1, 1.00:1, 0.770:1 (0.732:1 on V8i models), reverse 3.536:1.

Optional ZF 4HP22 HE automatic gearbox; gear ratios as on 1994-1998 models.
Two-speed LT230Q transfer gearbox; gear ratios 1.211:1 (High range) and 3.269:1 (Low range).
Front and rear final drive ratios as on 1994-1998 models.

Steering, suspension and brakes:
Steering as on 1994-1998 models.
Front suspension as on 1994-1998 models but with twin-tube hydraulic telescopic dampers.
Live rear axle with progressive-rate coil springs and twin-tube hydraulic telescopic dampers, located by radius arms and Watts linkage. Self-levelling air springs replace coil springs when ACE system fitted. Front and rear anti-roll bars standard, and linked to ACE system when fitted.
Disc brakes with 11.81in (300mm) diameter on all four wheels, with ventilated rotors at the front; vacuum servo assistance; dual hydraulic circuit on front wheels. Internal expanding drum-type parking brake operating on transfer box output shaft.
16-inch alloy wheels with 235/70 x 16 or 255/65 x 16 tyres; 215 x 16 tyres optional; 18-inch alloy wheels with 255 x 18 tyres optional.

Dimensions:

Wheelbase	100in (2,540mm)
Front track	60.6in (1,540mm)
Rear track	61.4in (1,560mm)
Length	185.2in (4,705mm)
Width	70.6in (1,793mm) over door mirrors
Height	76.4in (1,940mm) without roof bars
Kerb weight	4,453lb (2,020kg), V8i with five seats and all-coil suspension
	4,861lb (2,205kg), Td5 with seven seats and ACE system
Turning circle	39ft (11.9m)

APPENDIX B
CHASSIS NUMBER SEQUENCES

All Discovery models are identified by a VIN (Vehicle Identification Number), which consists of an 11-digit prefix code followed by a six-digit serial number. The prefixes used on US-specification vehicles (including those for Canada) differ from those used in other markets.

A typical non-US Discovery VIN on a pre-1999 model would be SALLJGBF7GA385697 (which was actually one of the 1989 launch press vehicles). This breaks down into 10 groups, SA-L-LJ-G-B-F-7-G-A-385697, which decode as follows:

1. SA   World manufacturer code for Rover Group.
2. L   Manufacturer sub-division for Land Rover.
3. LJ   Model code for Discovery.
4. G   First type code.   D = Honda Crossroad
                              G = standard 100-inch wheelbase
5. B   Second type code.   B = 3-door body
                              M = 5-door body
6. F   Engine type code.   F = Tdi intercooled turbodiesel
                              L = 3.5-litre injected petrol V8
                              M = 3.9-litre injected petrol V8
                              V = 3.5-litre carburettor V8
                              Y = 2-litre injected petrol four-cylinder
7. 7   Steering and transmission code.

                              3 = RHD automatic
                              4 = LHD automatic
                              7 = RHD 5-speed manual
                              8 = LHD 5-speed manual
8. G   Model-year or variant code.
                              G = 1990 model-year
                              H = 1991 model-year
                              J = 1992 model-year
                              K = 1993 model-year
                              L = 1994 model-year
                              M = 1995 model-year
                              N = 1996 model-year
                              P = 1997 model-year
                              R = 1998 model-year
                              S = 1999 model-year
9. A   Assembly location (Solihull).
10. 385697   Serial number.

(US VIN codes)

R = 1994 model-year
S = 1995 model-year
T = 1996 model-year
V = 1997 model-year
W = 1998 model-year

From the start of the 1999 model-year, the system changed, and the new codes are as follows:
1. SA World manufacturer code for Rover Group.
2. L Manufacturer sub-division for Land Rover.
3. LT Model code for New Discovery.
4. G First type code. A = Japanese market
G = Standard
5. M Second type code. M = 5-door body
6. 1 Engine type code. 1 = V8 for Australia
2 = V8 for EEC and Japan

3 = V8 for rest of world
7 = Td5 for all countries except:
9 = Td5 for Australia, EEC and Japan
7. 7 Steering and transmission code.
3 = RHD automatic
4 = LHD automatic
7 = RHD manual
8 = LHD manual
8. X Model-year code. X = 1999
Y = 2000
1 = 2001
9. A Assembly location A = Solihull
10. 123456 Serial number.

APPENDIX C
PRODUCTION TOTALS

The figures given in the following table are for calendar-year, not for model-year.

Model-year sales in the USA and Canada.

			USA	Canada
1989	3,296	1994	4,033	-
1990	23,067	1995	10,552	819
1991	19,261	1996	17,700	620
1992	24,347	1997	14,545	762
1993	35,558	1998	11,890	778
1994	54,499	(Projected figures only)		
1995	69,919			
1996	65,039			
1997	58,352 **(353,338 to the end of 1997)**			

APPENDIX D
DISCOVERY PERFORMANCE FIGURES

i) 1989-1994 models

	3-door Tdi manual	3-door V8 manual	5-door V8i manual
Max speed (mph)	92	95	105
Acceleration (sec)			
0-30mph	4.7	3.8	3.4
0-40mph	7.6	5.9	5.5
0-50mph	11.5	8.7	8.2
0-60mph	17.1	12.8	11.7
0-70mph	25.1	17.9	15.8
0-80mph	37.1	25.1	21.8
0-90mph	-	38.5	30.5
Standing ¼-mile (sec)	20.5	18.8	17.7
Direct top gear (sec)			
10-30mph	15.4	11.7	10.0
20-40mph	11.3	10.4	9.0
30-50mph	9.7	9.7	8.7
40-60mph	11.0	10.4	9.3
50-70mph	14.3	11.7	10.3
60-80mph	21.3	13.9	11.5
70-90mph	-	21.4	-
Overall fuel consumption (mpg)	23.9	14.0	16.5
Kerb weight (lb)	4432	4145	4152
Source	*Autocar & Motor* *Nov 15, 1989*	*Autocar & Motor* *Jan 3, 1990*	*Autocar & Motor* *Oct 17, 1990*

(ii) 1995-1998 models

	Mpi	Tdi manual	Tdi auto	V8i manual	V8i auto
Max speed (mph)	98	91	90	106	105
Acceleration (sec)					
0-30mph	4.7	4.7	4.8	3.7	3.9
0-40mph	7.3	7.8	8.1	5.2	5.9
0-50mph	10.4	11.8	12.0	7.8	6.6
0-60mph	15.3	17.2	18.9	10.8	11.8
0-70mph	21.0	24.7	20.0	14.8	16.1
0-80mph	30.2	36.5	45.2	19.8	21.9
0-90mph	48.5	-	-	26.6	28.9
Standing ¼-mile (sec)	20.3	20.8	21.3	17.9	18.7
Direct top gear (sec)					
10-30mph	-	-	-	-	-
20-40mph	-	-	-	-	-
30-50mph	12.5	10.3	-	8.3	-
40-60mph	13.3	11.0	-	8.2	-
50-70mph	15.2	13.1	-	8.6	-
60-80mph	18.7	10.1	-	9.7	-
70-90mp	-	-	-	-	-
Overall fuel consumption (mpg)*	19.5/ 32.0/ 23.9	32.8/ 42.9/ 28.2	30.5/ 44.2/ 30.0	13.7/ 27.5/ 20.5	14.0/ 27.4/ 20.2
Source	Land Rover	Land Rover	Land Rover	Land Rover	Land Rover

* Figures are for Urban consumption/ Constant 56mph/ Constant 75mph

(iii) 1998 and later models

	V8i manual	V8i auto	Td5 manual	Td5 auto
Max speed (mph)	106	106	98	98
Acceleration (sec)				
0-30mph	3.6	3.9	4.1	4.3
0-40mph				
0-50mph				
0-60mph	10.9	11.9	14.2	15.8
0-70mph				
0-80mph				
0-90mph				
0-100mph	39.2	45.7	-	-
Standing ¼-mile (sec)	18.1	18.7	19.7	20.3
Direct top gear (sec)				
10-30mph				
20-40mph				
30-50mph	8.4		8.5	
40-60mph				
50-70mph	9.2		10.9	
60-80mph				
70-90mph				
Overall fuel consumption (mpg)*	17.0	16.9	30.1	27.4
Source	Land Rover	Land Rover	Land Rover	Land Rover

*Combined figure obtained under EEC rules.